JOE PAPROCKI, DMin.

LIVING THE
SACRAMENTS

FINDING GOD AT THE
INTERSECTION OF
HEAVEN AND EARTH

LOYOLAPRESS.
A JESUIT MINISTRY
Chicago

LOYOLA PRESS.
A JESUIT MINISTRY

3441 N. Ashland Avenue
Chicago, Illinois 60657
(800) 621-1008
www.loyolapress.com

In accordance with c. 827, permission to publish is granted on May 30, 2018, by Very Reverend Ronald A. Hicks, Vicar General of the Archdiocese of Chicago. Permission to publish is an official declaration of ecclesiastical authority that the material is free from doctrinal and moral error. No legal responsibility is assumed by the grant of this permission.

Cover and interior design by Loyola Press
Cover art credit: mustafaU/iStock/Getty Images

Cartoons by Leighton Drake
Cartoons © 2018 Loyola Press

p. 76 By Frederick George Cotman, *One of the Family*, via Wikimedia Commons
p. 116 By William Ely Hill (1887–1962), *Puck*, 6. Nov 1915, via Wikimedia Commons

Scripture quotations are from Revised Standard Version of the Bible—Second Catholic Edition (Ignatius Edition) Copyright © 2006 National Council of the Churches of Christ in the United States of America. Used by permission. All rights reserved.

ISBN-13: 978-0-8294-4659-3
Library of Congress Control Number: 2018947269

Printed in the United States of America
18 19 20 21 22 23 24 25 26 27 28 LSC 10 9 8 7 6 5 4 3 2 1

DEDICATION

I dedicate this book to Joe and Maryann Sodini, with whom Joanne and I have been and continue to be privileged to share so many "thin moments" in a "thin place" known as Center Lake, WI.

Other Loyola Press Books by Joe Paprocki

The Catechist's Toolbox: How to Thrive
as a Religious Education Teacher

A Well-Built Faith: A Catholic's Guide to
Knowing and Sharing What We Believe

The Bible Blueprint: A Catholic's Guide to
Understanding and Embracing God's Word

Living the Mass: How One Hour a Week Can
Change Your Life (with Fr. Dominic Grassi)

Practice Makes Catholic: Moving from
a Learned Faith to a Lived Faith

Beyond the Catechist's Toolbox: Catechesis That
Not Only Informs but Also Transforms

7 Keys to Spiritual Wellness: Enriching Your Faith
by Strengthening the Health of Your Soul

Under the Influence of Jesus: The Transforming
Experience of Encountering Christ

The Catechist's Backpack: Spiritual Essentials
for the Journey

A Church on the Move: 52 Ways to Get
Mission and Mercy in Motion

CONTENTS

ACKNOWLEDGMENTS

I would like to thank the following people: Leighton Drake for his outstanding, creative, and whimsical cartoons that embellish this book; Jack Shea for introducing me to the notion of finding God at the intersection of heaven and earth; D. Todd Williamson for teaching me how to see mystagogically; Joe Durepos for not giving up on the idea of my writing a book on the sacraments; Rosemary Lane, Vinita Hampton Wright, and Beth Renaldi for exquisite editing; Donna Antkowiak for the engaging design of this book; Carrie Freyer for relentless promotion of all of my books; Maureen Kuhn for years of wise and compassionate spiritual direction; my parents for providing me with a healthy narrative within which to live the gift of life; the catechists, teachers, parents, and RCIA ministers who so lovingly prepare so many people—children and adults—to encounter Jesus in the sacraments; those clergy who preside at our sacramental celebrations with a deep recognition of the profound mystery that is taking place; all those disciples of Christ whose anointing has rubbed off on me; and my wife, Jo, for coloring my world since our first date in 1976.

INTRODUCTION: THIN MOMENTS

The ultimate human question is twofold: where is God, and is God accessible in my life?

Since the dawn of time, human beings have been in search of God and the means to commune with the divine. In some traditions (Celtic spirituality, for example), certain locations have been identified as spaces where God's presence is heightened and therefore more easily encountered. These spaces are referred to as "thin spaces," referring to the belief that God's presence is normally veiled from human awareness except for certain places where that veil seems to be quite thin.

> **The ultimate human question is twofold: where is God, and is God accessible in my life?**

Such thin spaces are usually majestic vistas of natural scenery: mountains, canyons, waterfalls, forests, rivers, oceans, and so on. While such places may indeed make us more aware of God's presence, they are not places where God is located per se. I may, for example, be perched on the most incredible mountaintop surrounded by miles of lush forests and streams, witnessing a stunning sunset. However, if at that very moment, I am consumed with nausea because of my fear of heights, burning with a fever from a virus I've caught, and wincing in pain from a toothache, I am not going to encounter God in that space. By the same token, I can be confined in the most mundane of settings with all of the above physical symptoms and hear a bird singing sweetly in the distance and recognize God's presence.

Thus, it seems to me that it is more fitting to speak of "thin moments" rather than "thin spaces." Christians believe that God, who transcends creation and cannot be contained within it, can be encountered in our experience and interaction with creation. Catholics, in particular, hold that God can be encountered in every moment of our lives if we have trained our spiritual senses to recognize God's presence around us. St. Ignatius of Loyola, the founder of the Jesuits, spoke of "finding God in all things," meaning that, with the right set of eyes, we should be able to experience these thin moments when we are aware of God's presence at any time, in any place, and in any experience. These thin moments are when we recognize that we are metaphorically standing at the intersection of heaven and earth—not a physical location but a reality in which God's presence oozes forth, coating every aspect of our human existence with divine residue.

The Intersection of Heaven and Earth

For Christians, Jesus Christ himself *is* the intersection of heaven and earth—the marriage of divinity and humanity. Jesus is the Sacrament of God, the tangible embodiment of the intangible God. Since his Ascension and the coming of the Holy Spirit, Jesus has given his followers tangible signs of his own intangible presence. He's given us the sacraments: those thin moments when we find ourselves encountering and keenly aware of the divine presence. Catholics number these thin moments—these sacraments—as seven. God's presence and grace are not somehow magically harnessed or limited to these sacramental objects and actions. Rather, God—who is with us always—speaks and acts directly in and through these sacramental rites. God's presence is experienced in a heightened way in both the ritual and in the divine residue that lingers after the celebration of the sacrament.

> **As Catholics, our quest is not just to receive the sacraments but to live the sacraments.**

As Catholics, our quest is not just to receive the sacraments but to live the sacraments. The sacraments represent a way of life for us Catholics. It was no accident that the first Christians were called followers of "the Way." Christians were seen as embracing what St. Ignatius later referred to as a "way of proceeding"—a modus operandi, so to speak. The Christian "M.O." was and is sacramental; it's a way of living in which one seeks to recognize every encounter and experience of life as a potential thin moment and an opportunity to encounter God.

To be Catholic is to permanently plant oneself at the intersection of heaven and earth—a vantage point that enables us to see humanity and divinity as inseparably and eternally intertwined. The sacraments continuously lead us toward that intersection, as opposed to the many avenues and detours we too often traverse that result in dead ends. Thus, this book is nothing less than a road map for discovering the answer to the questions that we began with: Where is God? (very near to us) And, is God accessible in my life? (Yes, yes, and again, yes!)

A Key to Reading This Book

It is not uncommon for mapmakers to provide a map legend or key that visually explains the various symbols found in the map. Such a legend helps one correctly read and interpret the map. In a similar way, I would like to provide you with a legend or key for how to best read this book. In the genre of literature, we call this key a *hermeneutic*: a method of interpreting. But first, let me tell you what this book is not. It is not a work of apologetics on the seven sacraments of the Church; it does not seek to defend or prove the truth of the sacraments through some type of systematic argumentation. Likewise, it is not a systematic theological exploration of the sacraments or a rubrical guide to celebrating the sacraments properly. Those three types of approaches, while valuable and much needed, are not my forte, nor do I think they are what is most needed at this time in the life of the Church for the average person.

The key to reading this book is to see it as an invitation to *mystagogy* (MISS-tuh-gah-ghee), a word that means "leading one through mystery." It is an invitation to a new way of thinking and a new way of seeing by finding God in all things. If you read this book with a mystagogical lens, you will come away with a whole new understanding of the sacraments: not as a once-and-done isolated event or milestone but as a spiritual path for encountering God in everyday life. God is in our midst, and he can truly be experienced by those who choose to follow the "Way," the sacramental mode of living that enables us to find God in all things.

> To be Catholic is to permanently plant oneself at the intersection of heaven and earth—a vantage point that enables us to see humanity and divinity as inseparably and eternally intertwined.

So, put on your mystagogical lens and prepare to read this book not like a textbook but as if you were listening to the words of a tour guide at a natural wonder or a docent at an art museum. This tour will invite you to take in the beauty and mystery of an awesome reality you may not fully comprehend or appreciate but feel compelled to stare at for as long as you'd like.

Chapter 1

Learning to Read Signs: Speaking God's Language

"Great is the mystery of the faith!" This mystery, then, requires that the faithful believe in it, that they celebrate it, and that they live from it in a vital and personal relationship with the living and true God. (*Catechism of the Catholic Church*, no. 2558)

What Really Makes It Better?

It is very common for a child with an ouchie to ask Mommy or Daddy to "kiss it and make it better." I seriously doubt that you will find a mom or dad who would refuse to do so if asked by their child. In fact, if you were to ask any parent if this approach really "works," I'm sure they would say yes. I know I would.

Now, those same parents (including me) would clarify that we do not believe that the act of kissing a scrape, bump, cut, or bruise actually has a clinically observable healing effect. And yet, we would still hold true that kissing the aforementioned boo-boo makes it better because we know that symbolic acts such as hugging, giving flowers, embracing, holding hands, and even smiling have an effect on human beings. Symbolic or ritual actions and objects can be thought of as the enactments or embodiments of a narrative: simply put, they tell a story. When a child falls and scrapes

"Your father has an honorary degree in Daddy Medicine."

a knee, he or she enters into an experience—a narrative—that is unfamiliar: pain and fear. When Mommy or Daddy kisses the scrape, the child is brought back into a familiar narrative: one in which the child knows he or she is loved, cared for, protected, and accompanied by a parent who will not let the pain prevail. As a result, the child feels comforted, gains strength and courage, and even learns to laugh at the event. Kissing it really does make it better.

> **Symbolic or ritual actions and objects can be thought of as the enactments or embodiments of a narrative: simply put, they tell a story.**

All ritual actions accomplish the same result: they enact a narrative. And while most rituals and symbols are performed to invoke positive narratives, some do not. Symbolic actions such as displaying a Confederate flag, a swastika, or a burning cross invoke painful narratives of enslavement, oppression, and the extermination of human beings. Symbols and rituals tell a story.

Hollow Gestures

If a ritual action becomes disengaged from its narrative, it no longer invokes a story and becomes a hollow gesture, a routine or superstition. In other words, a ritual must be connected to a story so that the act of performing it immediately invokes the story. So what narrative does the sacramental life of the Church invoke? One need look no further than the Nicene Creed that we recite at Mass, in which we proclaim that Jesus Christ, "the Only Begotten Son of God . . . came down from heaven . . . became man . . . was crucified under Pontius Pilate . . . suffered death and was buried . . . rose again on the third day . . . ascended into heaven . . . [and] will come again in glory." You are also, no doubt, familiar with a shorter version of this narrative, found in one of the most popular Gospel verses of all time: "For God so loved the world that he sent his only Son, so that those who believe in him might not perish but might have eternal life." (John 3:16)

> **"Symbols can be so beautiful, sometimes."**
> —KURT VONNEGUT,
> *BREAKFAST OF CHAMPIONS*

Knowing Our Christian Narrative

In simple terms, the Christian narrative can be summed up with three Rs:

➕ **Rescue**—The story of salvation history is a story of God rescuing his people from bondage: first, from the bondage of slavery in Egypt and, eventually, from the bondage of sin through the life, Death, and Resurrection of Jesus Christ.

➕ **Restoration**—God continually restores us to right relationship with him and with one another.

➕ **Reassurance**—God's saving grace continues to be present to us through the presence of the Holy Spirit and the Church and, in particular, the sacraments.

That's it. That's our narrative. We live our lives within the context of this good news: we are rescued, restored, and reassured. Every time we pour water, anoint with oil, lay our hands over someone, light a fire, break bread, make the Sign of the Cross, pray the Rosary, or put on a scapular, this is the narrative we Catholics are invoking—one that stands in opposition to the all-too-prevalent realities of pain and loss, emptiness and brokenness, and isolation and loneliness that often creep into our lives like seepage through a crack in the foundation of our home.

The Christian narrative, which shapes the direction of our lives, is an "alternative ending" to a story that appears to be hopelessly and wildly progressing toward a tragic ending. The Christian narrative is the ultimate director's cut, as it represents how God intends the story to end. Thus, the most effective way of proclaiming the Good News is to present it as a response to bad news.

> **We live our lives within the context of this good news: we are rescued, restored, and reassured.**

1. **The Bad News:** We human beings are broken and in need of fixing. We are incapable of sustaining ourselves or of overcoming sin on our own.

2. **The Good News:** God has intervened to rescue us by becoming one of us through his Son, Jesus Christ, who defeated sin and death through his cross and Resurrection and restored us to a life of grace. Jesus invites us to begin sharing now in eternal life and reassures us of his ongoing presence through the Holy Spirit and the Church so that we might enjoy new life (grace) as his disciples.

Every sacrament of the Church, every ritual, every sacramental object tells this story and enacts this narrative. A ritual action that fails to do this rings hollow. On the other hand, those ritual actions that invoke this narrative most powerfully remain the most popular practices for Catholics throughout the ages.

Finding God in Our Midst

As someone who wears glasses, I understand what it means to look at the world through a lens. The truth is, we all view the world through a specific lens that we have been conditioned to rely on. This lens shapes our thoughts, words, and actions. The Catholic lens is shaped by our Christian narrative. At the heart of this narrative is the reality of the Incarnation of Jesus Christ—the incredibly good news that God chose to dwell among his people. God's nearness is what we human beings desire most, especially when life leads us to believe that we are alone, abandoned, unloved, uncared for, or perhaps even forgotten. Like any loving parent, God has made himself present to his children: he chose to enter into the physical world that he created and took on flesh that was embodied in Jesus. The invisible God became visible: Jesus was and is the "Sacrament of God" (Edward Schillebeeckx, *Christ the Sacrament of the Encounter with God*), the tangible, visible sign of an intangible, invisible reality.

> God's nearness is what we human beings desire most.

The Catholic vision, then, is one that recognizes God as being present in the world—a sacramental vision. According to St. Ignatius, if we human beings adjust our vision, we should be able to find and recognize God in all things. This lens inspired Jesuit priest and poet Gerard Manley Hopkins to write his classic poem "God's Grandeur":

> The world is charged with the grandeur of God.
>   It will flame out, like shining from shook foil;
>   It gathers to a greatness, like the ooze of oil
> Crushed. Why do men then now not reck his rod?
> Generations have trod, have trod, have trod;
>   And all is seared with trade; bleared, smeared with toil;
>   And wears man's smudge and shares man's smell: the soil
> Is bare now, nor can foot feel, being shod.

And for all this, nature is never spent;
    There lives the dearest freshness deep down things;
And though the last lights off the black West went
    Oh, morning, at the brown brink eastward, springs—
Because the Holy Ghost over the bent
    World broods with warm breast and with ah! bright wings.

The Catholic sacramental vision is fueled by its narrative. In other words, the Christian narrative that centers on the presence of God among his people and within his creation allows us to see "deep down things"—namely, God's presence reflected in the beauty of the earth and in nature. God chose to reveal his presence to his people using various aspects of nature: a brushfire, a column of smoke, a pillar of fire, a whispering wind, a mighty wind, tongues of fire. The Catholic lens, then, enables us to see God revealed in all things. We have a sacramental worldview, meaning that we see God revealed in natural things such as water, oil, bread, wine, fire, human touch, human gestures, and human words. While we recognize both the immanence and transcendence of God, the Catholic worldview leans scandalously in the direction of God's nearness to us. As my friend and liturgist extraordinaire D. Todd Williamson is fond of saying, "God did not visit Planet Earth, stay for a while, and then depart! Rather, he became what he created: human!"

> **While we recognize both the immanence and transcendence of God, the Catholic worldview leans scandalously in the direction of God's nearness to us.**

God Is Accessible

The incarnation is God's profound way of reminding us how accessible his loving presence and divine will is:

> "It is not up in heaven, so that you have to ask, 'Who will ascend into heaven to get it and proclaim it to us so we may obey it?' Nor is it beyond the sea, so that you have to ask, 'Who will cross the sea to get it and proclaim it to us so we may obey it?' No, the word is very near you; it is in your mouth and in your heart so you may obey it."
>
> –Deuteronomy 30:12-14

Through the Holy Spirit and the sacraments of the Church, Jesus Christ, the living Word of God, continues to be very near to us—not just in one geographical location as when he walked the earth two thousand years ago but throughout the entire world. The presence of God, while very real, is equally mysterious.

Understanding Mystery

In contemporary culture, a mystery is something to be solved. In biblical tradition, however, a mystery is something to be entered into, something to stand in awe of. In essence, a mystery is something hidden that is revealed and yet remains hidden. Even though God has revealed himself to us throughout all of salvation history, culminating in the pinnacle of his revelation, Jesus Christ, God still remains beyond our grasp. We can encounter God. We can know God. But we cannot solve God. We experience God in those thin moments that pass all too quickly, seemingly surrounded by a fog that prevents us from seeing with precision.

Another contemporary understanding of mystery is to refer to something that is incomprehensible. When we Catholics hear about the mystery of our faith, the Paschal Mystery of Jesus, the mystery of the Trinity, or the mysteries of the Rosary, we may mistakenly think that we are called either to solve these mysteries or to dismiss them as beyond our understanding. If this is the case, then, when the priest invites us to proclaim "the mystery of faith" after the Consecration at Mass, he is inviting us to proclaim something that none of us understands. The fact is, we cannot solve the mystery of faith, and we may not fully understand it, but we can know it in the same way that we can know a spouse, child, parent, sibling, or close friend and yet be unable to explain or fully understand that person.

> **The mystery at the heart of our faith is that from death comes new life. We do not fully understand this. We cannot solve this. But we know in our heart of hearts that from death comes new life. Death is not the end.**

In every fiber of our being, we do know the mystery of our faith: the almighty and ever-living God became one of us, died to save us, rose, and will come again. This is the essence of the central mystery of our faith: the Paschal Mystery of Jesus. The word *paschal* comes from the Greek word for Passover, when the Hebrew people were saved by the blood of the lamb. We, in turn, are saved by the blood of the Lamb of God, Jesus, who is our Passover, our Pasch—thus, Paschal Mystery. The mystery at the heart of our faith is that from death comes new life. We do not fully understand this. We cannot solve this. But we know in our heart of hearts that from death comes new life. Death is not the end.

Learning the Language of Mystery

When God revealed his mysterious presence to Moses, he did so in a way that Moses could understand. Moses was a shepherd and, on any given day at "the office," he could witness a brushfire. On this occasion, however, something mysterious happened: the bush was on fire, but it wasn't consumed. Like any normal human being who is confronted with mystery, Moses experienced approach-avoidance conflict: he was compelled to explore more closely but with a sense of caution or even fear. Notice, however, that Moses' encounter began without a word uttered. God revealed his presence through a natural phenomenon with a mysterious twist. Even when God finally spoke to Moses, he did not ask Moses to say anything. Rather, he asked him to remove his sandals as an expression of reverence. God enters into the lives of his people through signs and symbols that point to his presence, that enable us to encounter and know him and yet not fully comprehend or solve the mystery of God's essence. The Catholic Church did not invent signs and symbols as a form of encountering the Divine. God did.

Human beings recognize that in the most profound moments of life, words come up short. Some years after the atrocities of World War II, the mayor of Berlin, Willy Brandt, visited a memorial in Poland to victims of the Warsaw Ghetto Uprising. Upon approaching the memorial, Brandt fell to his knees and bowed his head in silence. When asked later to explain the gesture, Brandt said, "This gesture was not planned. I simply did what people do when words fail them" (Willy Brandt, *People and Politics*). Such is the human response in the face of an encounter with the Divine. Words fail us. We Catholics are a sacramental people, expressing ourselves beyond words and relying on signs, symbols, and ritual gestures because this is how

> **Human beings recognize that in the most profound moments of life, words come up short.**

human beings express themselves in the face of mystery. Human beings know that words alone are not enough, especially in relationships. When it comes to the most profound moments of life, we engage our entire bodies in expressing ourselves to God, who himself speaks to us in ways that transcend words.

For Catholics, sacramentality is a language; it relies on signs, symbols, rituals, and gestures to express our encounters with God. Ultimately, sacramentality deals with the question "Where do you find God?" For some, God is a distant reality. Not so for Catholics. We believe that God can be found in all things and yet still remains a mystery. We do not equate the natural world with God (pantheism), nor do we believe that God is a distant reality (deism). Rather, we believe that the natural world is a reflection of God's transcendent presence and that all of God's creation is a channel of grace. We can call this way of seeing reality the Catholic sacramental sensibility.

"If you could say it in words, there would be no reason to paint."
—EDWARD HOPPER

Ordinary Things

Because of our sacramental sensibility, it's no surprise that when we celebrate our encounters with God in the seven sacraments, we use ordinary things from the natural world, such as water, oil, fire, bread, and wine, as channels of God's grace. By the same token, we are very comfortable using

Former President George W. Bush had a dream that he died and went to heaven, where he was greeted by all the saints, martyrs, and prophets, except for Moses, who turned and walked away. Later, President Bush caught up with Moses and said, "Excuse me, Moses. Why did you walk away from me? Do you know who I am?" Moses replied, "Sure I do. You're former President George W. Bush." The former president was happy to be recognized but pressed further, "Then why did you walk away from me?" Moses replied, "Last time I spoke to a bush, my people got lost and starved for 40 years!"

images and objects to assist us in our prayers and devotions. For Catholics, statues, holy cards, icons, rosaries, crucifixes, and other sacred images, which are referred to as sacramentals, draw our attention to God's mysterious presence. We know full well that when we pray before a statue, we are not praying to or worshiping the statue. We certainly do not believe the statue is the manifestation of God or Mary or the saints. Rather, we use the images as reminders of God's grace and mysterious presence in this world.

In these moments when we experience the divine, words are not the primary form of expression. Catholics are more at home with a language of mystery that relies less on an alphabet and more on expressions that speak to and prod the imagination. So, what are the elements of this language of mystery? Let's take a quick look.

✚ **Sign and Symbol**—At the intersection of heaven and earth, a type of sign language is spoken. As we mentioned, God revealed his presence to Moses through the sign of a burning bush. Signs and symbols speak directly to the heart, through the imagination. They invite rather than command, inspire rather than explain. We rely on visible, tangible signs (statues, icons, rosaries, medals, holy water) to seek strength from hidden, unseen graces and protection and deliverance from hidden, unseen dangers. (Examples in the liturgy and sacramental life include water, oil, fire, bread, white garments, wine, incense, statues, icons, and stained-glass windows.)

✚ **Ritual**—There is a fine line between routine and ritual. A routine is something we do the same way habitually with little or no thought. Every morning, we mindlessly follow a routine: turn off the alarm, turn on the coffeepot, eat a bowl of cereal, brush our teeth, and so on. A ritual is something we do the same way habitually, with deep, intentional thought. Blessing ourselves with holy water, genuflecting, anointing with oil, walking in procession—these are all examples of ritual acts. If done without deep, intentional thought, they risk becoming routine. When done with deep, intentional thought, these ritual actions invoke the Christian narrative. At the intersection of heaven and earth, rituals abound. They connect us with meaningful events in our past (rescue), they ground us in the present (restoration), and they lead us confidently into the future (reassurance). Rituals awaken a deeper level of consciousness within us. They remind us that we are truly at home in that special place where the spirit dwells. (Examples from liturgy and sacramental life include sprinkling rites, anointings, blessings, ritual dialogue, laying on of hands, and putting on a white garment.)

➕ **Movement and Gesture**—When non-Catholics experience Catholic liturgy for the first time, they often comment on how we Catholics seem to be constantly in motion as we worship: we sit, stand, kneel, cross ourselves, bow, and walk in procession. This motion is not mind-less, like hamsters on a wheel, but intentional, like dancers on a stage. In worship, we move about prayerfully, as though every movement is saying something. These controlled movements connect body, mind, and spirit based on the belief that what happens to one affects the others. When we use our bodies for prayerful movement and gesture, the mind hears and the heart responds. (Examples from liturgy and sacramental life include making the Sign of the Cross, processions, bowing, and genuflecting.)

➕ **Silence**—When encountering thin moments, one discovers that the primary form of expression is silence. Thomas Keating, a Trappist monk, tells us, "Silence is God's first language; everything else is a poor translation. In order to hear that language, we must learn to be still and to rest in God" (*Invitation to Love*). We live in a world that shuns silence and seeks to fill every empty space with sound. As a result, we become divorced from God's whisper. (Examples from liturgy and sac-ramental life include the silence before Mass, after the Scripture readings, after the homily, and after Communion.)

> **At the intersection of heaven and earth, one discovers that the primary form of expression is silence.**

➕ **Song**—The music never stops at the intersection of heaven and earth! Few things can touch our hearts and transport our minds better than music and song. This must be why the Psalms refer to music so often—almost a hundred times, in fact. "O sing to the Lord a new song," the psalmist urges us (96:1). Lucky for us, God loves music and loves to hear us sing. The most powerful songs of our Christian tradition are those that not only lift our hearts but also retell the narrative of our salvation. They catechize us. I have long insisted that if some "Grinch" came along and absconded with all the catechetical textbooks and catechisms of the Catholic faith, we would still be able to effectively form disciples of Jesus as long as we had access to hymnals! (Examples include hymns and sung parts of Mass.)

➕ **Storytelling**—At the intersection of heaven and earth, it is always story time. Approximately one-third of the recorded sayings of Jesus take the form of parables. The man could tell a story! He knew that stories create worlds and new realities that we can envision and enter into. Jesus' stories tap into our imaginations, compelling us to consider the possibility of an alternate reality—a new narrative. Author John Shea tells us that "story is the most interesting and compelling of language forms" and that "storytelling raises us out of the randomness of the moment and inserts us into a larger framework"

Thin Moments: The Language of Mystery

Like any language, the language of mystery can be lost if not practiced regularly. You can practice the language of mystery in your daily life in these small ways.

> Sign and Symbol—Choose one symbol (a crucifix, an icon, or a medal) that you will see first thing each morning to remind you of God's nearness throughout the day.
> Ritual—Establish your own daily prayer ritual. For example, light a candle; sit quietly for a few minutes and breathe deeply with your eyes closed; trace the Sign of the Cross with your thumb on your forehead, lips, and chest as you pray that God be in your head, on your lips, and in your heart; hold a small crucifix in your hands as you pray for the needs of others.
> Movement and Gesture—Gently bow your head in the direction of the rising sun to remind yourself to direct your full attention to the Lord each day.
> Silence—Set aside several minutes of complete silence and solitude to allow God's grace to surround you.
> Song—Play at least one song of praise each day on your favorite music device.
> Storytelling—Every day, tell someone about a moment of grace you experienced: a sunrise, a kind smile, a meaningful encounter, a moment of joy.

(*Stories of Faith*). That larger framework is the kingdom of God, and we all have a part to play in it. Storytelling is one of the primary vehicles for conveying the Christian narrative that shapes our vision of life, others, ourselves, and God. (Examples include Scripture readings, the homily, stained-glass windows, and sacred art.)

The language of mystery that is spoken at the intersection of heaven and earth predisposes us to the possibility of an alternate reality—a new narrative. The kingdom of God is, in fact, an alternate reality embedded within the one we can see and hear. We are called to enter into this reality by training our eyes, ears, and spirits to perceive the world anew. Knowing the language of mystery can help us answer the call. This is what faith formation is all about. If things were simply as they appeared, we would have no need for ongoing faith formation. However, life's ultimate meaning is veiled and mysterious. Therefore, we need faith formation in order to incorporate these various elements of the language of mystery into our souls' daily diet.

A New Narrative

At the time of the writing of this book, it was reported that Chester Bennington, the lead singer of the rock group Linkin Park, had committed suicide. In a radio interview that aired following his death, Chester talked about the difficulties he was struggling with, saying, "I don't know if anyone out there can relate, but I have a hard time with life. Sometimes it's great but a lot of times for me, it's really hard." He went on to talk about how the "skull between his ears" was a "bad neighborhood" and that it was very difficult for him to be "inside of himself." Like many people, Chester Bennington recognized that the narrative that directed his thoughts and actions was unhealthy and that it required much more than shaking it off or thinking positive thoughts to change that narrative. Too many of us are walking around with narratives that tell us that we are

+ worthless
+ ugly
+ fat
+ unlovable
+ shameful
+ inferior

+ untalented
+ unreliable
+ uninteresting
+ undeserving
+ incapable of happiness

... and that we need

- ⊕ money
- ⊕ power
- ⊕ possessions
- ⊕ pleasure
- ⊕ control

- ⊕ popularity
- ⊕ success
- ⊕ conquest
- ⊕ prestige
- ⊕ fame

In Search of a Healthy Narrative

What the Gospel offers, first and foremost, is a change of narrative. Too often, we reduce Jesus' call to repentance as a call to put aside bad habits. This approach causes us to focus on a laundry-list approach to repentance: if I stop swearing, watch my temper, and stop being envious of my neighbor, I'll be saved. What the Gospel is calling us to, however, is not simply a change of habits, but more importantly, a change in one's vision of life—a change in one's narrative. Too often, the Church has lost touch with this call to embrace a new narrative and has instead reduced the Gospel to a code of ethics that one must adhere to in order to measure up as a true Christian.

> **What the Gospel is calling us to, however, is not simply a change of habits, but more importantly, a change in one's vision of life—a change in one's narrative.**

It's no wonder many people feel that religion in general, and Christianity in particular, is unnecessary. Bad habits can be changed without all the trappings of organized religion. When people say that they are "spiritual but not religious," it often means that they are in search of a healthy narrative to guide their life, and they are not finding such a narrative in the institutional church, just judgment. The last thing we want when our car breaks down on the side of the road is for someone to drive by and shout out what we did wrong. What we all want and need is to be rescued, restored, and reassured. According to psychologist Eugene Taylor, "Personal testimonies to belief in a higher power are now regularly proclaimed, not from church pews, but in cancer support groups, meditation centers, and wellness treks, not to mention Alcoholics Anonymous and other 12-step groups" ("Desperately Seeking Spirituality," *Psychology Today*, Nov. 1, 1994).

These venues—in particular, 12-step groups—offer people a new narrative to replace the unhealthy narratives that are guiding their lives into disarray, unhappiness, and, in too many cases, ruin. Recovery from any form of addiction requires a healthy self-narrative, lest the "stinking thinking" that caused the addiction in the first place reassert itself. The Christian narrative tells us that we are born and live addicted to sin but that in Jesus Christ, we find a path to recovery and sobriety—to a new life that is also known as salvation. It is through the sacraments of the Church that we are continually called back to this life-saving narrative that reassures us of God's nearness and undying love for us.

> **The Christian narrative tells us that we are born and live addicted to sin but that in Jesus Christ, we find a path to recovery and sobriety—to a new life that is also known as salvation.**

Science, Logic, Reason . . . and Mystery

Recently, I saw a video that went viral on Facebook showing some teens ambushing and beating a fellow teen simply because she was Muslim. In the comments section, I came across the following comment: "Despicable! Religion is to blame. ALL religion is crap! Science, logic, reason . . . the only things that can be trusted!" While this sentiment is common today (in her book *iGen*, Professor Jean Twenge refers to members of the generation born in the mid-1990s and later as the least religious generation in American history), there are many reasons why it is problematic, not the least of which is the fact that this argument creates a false dichotomy between science and faith. And while the Church has been guilty at times of portraying science as an enemy, in truth, some of the greatest advocates of science were devoutly religious (including the scientist who formulated what came to be known as the Big Bang theory: a Belgian Catholic priest named Georges Henri Joseph Édouard Lemaître, who was an astronomer and physicist).

> **"Little science takes you away from God but more of it takes you to Him."**
> —LOUIS PASTEUR

That being said, there is much that science cannot measure or explain. Science will never be able to explain the meaning of a work of art, poetry, or literature. Science cannot define or explain beauty. Science will never be able to define goodness or joy. Science will never be able to explain the purpose of a human life. Science cannot explain what makes something funny or sad. Science cannot define what constitutes true love.

This is precisely why we say in the Nicene Creed that we believe God is the "maker of heaven and earth, of all things *visible and invisible*." We believe that God is the maker of all things empirical, which means we should study them in order to grow in our knowledge of God's remarkable creation. It also means, however, that we believe in a reality—in a truth—beyond the empirical; we believe in an unseen reality. Our models for this are the Magi, who came in search of the newborn king (as described in the Gospel of Matthew). They were astronomers, scientists who relied on science to point them to a deeper understanding of reality and truth. They saw science as something to explore and respect but God as "something" to bow before.

While science studies that which is rational and verifiable, this does not mean that faith is irrational or that faith experiences are unverifiable. That which is mystery isn't unknowable but rather "infinitely knowable." Our five senses are limited: they inform us of only a very small fraction of what we call reality. That which is unseen or invisible is not to be equated with imaginary. A true Catholic vision recognizes that both the seen reality (the visible) and the unseen reality (the invisible) are real; they do not exist side by side but are intimately connected and intertwined in the multilayered reality that is God's creation.

> "I believe in one God, the Father almighty, maker of heaven and earth, of all things visible and invisible."
> —Nicene Creed

The essence of sacramentality is belief in not only that which is seen/visible but also in that which is unseen/invisible. Thin places or moments are precisely those places and experiences in which we come to know that which is unseen or invisible. Welcome to the sacraments: the thin moments of our Catholic experience.

Scripture

For this reason I kneel before the Father, from whom every family in heaven and on earth derives its name. I pray that out of his glorious riches he may strengthen you with power through his Spirit in your inner being, so that Christ may dwell in your hearts through faith. And I pray that you, being rooted and established in love, may have power, together with all the Lord's holy people, to grasp how wide and long and high and deep is the love of Christ, and to know this love that surpasses knowledge—that you may be filled to the measure of all the fullness of God.   (EPHESIANS 3:14–19)

Prayer

Good and gracious God, reveal your invisible presence to me. Give me eyes to see your presence reflected in the visible realities of this world. Through the sacraments of your Church, tell me the stories of rescue, restoration, and reassurance. Help me gain deeper access to your loving and merciful presence. Teach me your language of mystery that I may encounter "deep-down things" such as your love and grace in all things visible and invisible. Grant me many thin moments in my daily living—moments in which your mystery is revealed and yet remains hidden. Amen.

Chapter 2

Living the Sacrament of Baptism: A Whole New You

Holy Baptism is the basis of the whole Christian life, the gateway to life in the Spirit and the door that gives access to the other sacraments. Through Baptism we are freed from sin and reborn as sons of God; we become members of Christ, are incorporated into the Church, and made sharers in her mission: "Baptism is the sacrament of regeneration through water in the word." (*Catechism of the Catholic Church*, no. 1213)

A Day of Liberation

June 19 may not seem like a significant date to some people. But for African Americans, June 19 is known as "Juneteenth," a celebration of the day in 1865 when word of the Emancipation Proclamation finally reached the Deep South, a full two and a half years after President Lincoln issued the executive order. Spontaneous and jubilant celebrations burst forth as men, women, and children who were previously enslaved under deplorable and oppressive conditions learned that they were liberated. To this day, African Americans celebrate Juneteenth to recall that glorious day when, at long last, they had a new narrative: one that was characterized not by the bondage of slavery but by the glorious freedom that is the inherent right of all human beings.

In much the same way, Baptism celebrates our liberation from a different kind of slavery: the power and dysfunction of sin. According to St. Paul, we who were once slaves of sin have been set free (Romans 6:16–22). At the heart of the Christian narrative is the belief that, powerless to free ourselves, we are totally reliant on the intervention of God's mercy and grace to save us from the destructive and oppressive power of sin. We cannot just declare our freedom from sin—that victory can only be achieved by God, who did so through his Son, Jesus Christ. The day we entered the waters of Baptism is the day of our liberation and a day to be recalled, cherished, and responded to with deep gratitude.

> **The day we entered the waters of Baptism is the day of our liberation.**

Embracing Powerlessness

We don't like to admit powerlessness because we tend to confuse powerlessness with weakness. I may have the strength and courage to resist an enemy, but if that enemy has effectively chained my hands and feet, I have been rendered powerless. According to the wisdom of 12-step groups, it is this embracing of our ultimate powerlessness that is a prerequisite for healing. Those of us who deal with debilitating addictions (or even minor addictions) can easily convince ourselves that we are capable of stopping at any time on our own. Twelve-step wisdom, however, requires the individual to admit powerlessness as a precursor to actual healing.

This admission of powerlessness is not an admission of weakness but a recognition of the oppressive force that has rendered our ability to resist futile. In Baptism, we admit powerlessness over sin and call on a higher power—the grace and mercy of God that we receive through Jesus Christ—to save us from ourselves. The healing we experience in Baptism, however, is not magical. Rather, like a participant in a 12-step program, it sets us on the correct path, surrounds us with the help we need to resist temptation and to avoid stinking thinking, provides us with healthy alternatives, and requires that we regularly attend meetings (the celebration of the Eucharist) that will enable us to successfully work the program for the remainder of our lives. It is no accident that the Sunday meeting we are called to participate in begins with the admission of our powerlessness over sin (the Penitential Act). I'll explain more about that in the chapter on the Eucharist (page 49).

> **"Do you renounce sin, so as to live in the freedom of the children of God?"**
> —Renewal of Baptismal Promises

Gaining Access

In many action movies, the good guy defeats the bad guy by gaining access to his or her computer. As the clock ticks down and our hero gets closer and closer to the files he or she needs to download, the inevitable request for a password or access code pops up. Of course, in Hollywood, the hero is always able to guess the password and, just before time runs out, gain access to the information that saves the day and defeats evil.

Baptism, which provides us access to intimacy with God, requires no secret code. We don't have to search for a way to gain access. That access has been revealed to us in the Person of Jesus Christ, who states very clearly, "I am the Way, and the Truth, and the Life" (John 14:6). We are told precisely how we can gain access to God's grace by choosing to live not in our own name but in the name of the Father, the Son, and the Holy Spirit. Although the formula for Baptism is not secret, it is specific. It requires the following:

- ✚ the decision to leave behind an old narrative of self-sufficiency in favor of a new narrative or way of living that relies on God to save us through the Person of Jesus Christ
- ✚ the pouring of water and the words "I baptize you in the name of the Father, and of the Son, and of the Holy Spirit. Amen."

Through this simple yet profound ritual, we are introduced to a relationship of love that will sustain us for the rest of our lives. Our work, however, is just beginning. Just as our hero who gained access to the enemy's computer now has to identify the correct files, download them, and figure out how to use the information to benefit others, our access to God's grace must be followed by the hard work of recognizing it, integrating it into our lives, and learning how to use it for the good of ourselves and others. While it is wonderful to have access to that which can benefit us, unless we know what we are looking for and how to use it, that access is a missed opportunity.

Embracing the Grace of God

When all is said and done, Baptism is ultimately about having our lives reformed and transformed by God, and this task is central to the Christian faith. The first words of Jesus' public ministry, according to the Gospel of Mark, are "The time has come. The kingdom of God has come near. Repent and believe the good news!" (Mark 1:15) *Repent* means to change,

The Liturgy of Baptism

The Rite of Baptism itself includes the following elements:

> The Sign of the Cross
> Readings from Scripture
> Exorcism and anointing
> Blessing the baptismal water
> Renunciation of sin and profession of faith
> Baptism with water and the words "I baptize you in the name of the Father, and of the Son, and of the Holy Spirit"
> Anointing with sacred chrism
> Reception of the white garment and the candle

reform, reshape, be transformed. Every year, Christians set aside forty days to focus on that task with greater intensity than during the rest of the year. The season of Lent exists because of one reason: people are preparing to receive the Sacrament of Baptism at the Easter Vigil.

When adults decide to reform their lives, turn away from sin, and embrace Jesus in Baptism, the Catholic Church walks with them on a journey of transformation called the catechumenate, also known as the RCIA (Rite of Christian Initiation of Adults). The catechumenate is a period of at least one year, during which time the catechumens—those preparing for Baptism—learn to leave behind sinful ways and follow the gospel message as taught by the Church. During the final forty days of their preparation for the Sacraments of Initiation, the entire Church prepares with them, seeking to once again reform our lives by rejecting sin and embracing the grace of God in Jesus Christ. It is a time for us to revisit our own Baptism and to renew it, to make it fresh and vibrant.

The Sacraments of Initiation

On Holy Saturday, at the Easter Vigil, the catechumens come forward to receive the Sacraments of Initiation. Although Baptism, Confirmation, and the Eucharist are distinct sacraments, they are inseparable from one another.

✚ Baptism is our entrance, through death, into a new narrative and new life in Jesus' Church.

✚ Confirmation seals us with the gift of the Holy Spirit.

✚ The Eucharist completes our initiation, bringing us to the table of the Lord, where we eat the Bread of Life and drink from the Cup of Eternal Salvation.

The dying and rising is complete. With our hearts melted and reformed by God's grace, we can say the words of St. Paul: "Yet I live, no longer I, but Christ lives in me" (Galatians 2:20).

Being Healed of Our Dysfunction

Any discussion of Baptism—or salvation, for that matter—must begin with the admission that we are, at our core, inherently dysfunctional. That is not to say that we are inherently evil. Rather, we are inherently good but hopelessly damaged and in need of repair. We human beings were created in factory condition to reflect the image of our Creator and to transmit the sweet strains of God's goodness, truth, and beauty. But we chose to seek another frequency, and in doing so, damaged ourselves. We call that dysfunction Original Sin.

To be born into the human family is to be born into dysfunction,

> "If the structures of the human mind remain unchanged, we will always end up re-creating the same world, the same evils, the same dysfunction."
> —ECKHART TOLLE

Upon coming out of the baptismal waters at the Easter Vigil, a young man, newly baptized, realized he had forgotten to remove his wallet from his trousers before entering the baptismal pool. He pulled his sopping-wet wallet out of his pocket and threw it at the priest, letting loose a string of expletives. When he was done venting, the priest lifted his arms to heaven and prayed, "Thank you, heavenly Father, for sending this young man to set such an excellent example for all of the baptized gathered here today!" The deacon gasped, "Father, how can you say that? His foul mouth and hot temper are a terrible example!" The priest replied, "Be that as it may, he *did* demonstrate what a Catholic is supposed to do with their wallet once they're baptized!"

not unlike the unfortunate fate of a child born with a debilitating condition inherited from his or her parents. There is no escaping that unfortunate inheritance without the intervention of a medical team. In Baptism, God's intervention, which cleanses and heals this dysfunction, is symbolized by the pouring of water—the washing clean of Original Sin.

Color My World

When I was a teenager, I started dating the young woman who has now been my wife since 1982. (You can do the math!) Fittingly enough, the theme for the fall dance that was our first date was "Color My World." Anyone who has fallen head over heels for someone, especially during adolescence, can attest to the effect that love has on your whole outlook. When I fell in love with Joanne, I quickly found that her love colored every aspect of my world. My heart beat a little faster not only when I saw her but also when I thought of her. Waking up knowing that I would see her later that day made the dark, cold Chicago mornings seem bright and warm. Even algebra class, which I hated with a passion, suddenly seemed, for the first time ever, to be endurable as long as I knew I would get to see my Jo later that evening. I couldn't wait to be in her presence, to see her face, to talk, hold hands, put my arm around her, kiss her, lay my head in her lap, and feel her fingers gently caress my face. When we parted ways at the end of the day, I could still smell her sweet fragrance on my collar where she had snuggled her head. I awakened each day to this new narrative. My world was colored by her love and, thankfully, still is to this day!

Baptism has a similar effect on us. When we encounter the beauty of God, we cannot help but fall in love with a love that colors our world. Even though our Baptism may have taken place many years ago, it never loses its effect as we continue to ponder, reflect on, and experience a love that overwhelms us and fills us with newness every day. This sentiment was captured by the psalmist: "On my bed I remember you; I think of you through the watches of the night" (Psalm 63:6). As we ponder the goodness of God, our heart beats

MEMORIES OF BAPTISM

"I don't remember much, but I'm told I was very emotional about it!"

a little faster with the knowledge that we are in the loving presence and embrace of God. We find ourselves eager to be in this presence, resting in God's tender embrace and experiencing God gently caressing our soul. Every time you allow your life to be colored by God, you are experiencing the fruits of Baptism—the beginning of a relationship that is forever young, forever fresh, forever new, and forever beautiful.

> **Every time you allow your life to be colored by God, you are experiencing the fruits of Baptism—the beginning of a relationship that is forever young, forever fresh, forever new, and forever beautiful.**

Adopted

I once saw an incredible video on YouTube that showed a ten-year-old boy's reaction on Christmas morning when he opened a gift from his adoptive parents that revealed a certificate that made his adoption final and official. The boy's first reaction is one of joy and happiness, and he reacts with a big smile but then continues to stare at the certificate. He cannot pull his gaze away from the words that officially seal his status as a member of the family and as a child of these loving parents, and his eyes quickly fill with tears of joy. He lunges into the arms of his father and sobs uncontrollably, knowing that he has a new narrative in which he is really and truly loved and that his standing as a member of this family is irrevocable.

St. Paul refers to us as adopted children of God through Baptism (Romans 8:15, 23; 9:4; Galatians 4:5; Ephesians 1:5). This may seem like a strange concept since we already believe that God is our Creator and Father. In the YouTube video, the boy was already living in the home of the people who, until that point, were his guardians. It was the action of the parents, however—the formalizing of a new relationship that was permanent and more intimate—that brought the boy to tears. It signaled the beginning of a whole new life: not one of being born but of being "born again" and redeemed. Adoption brings the assurance of security and a share in all the benefits of a familial relationship, including a new family narrative. It also brings the responsibility of living up to the new name that has been bestowed on us. It moves us from being creatures of God to children of God, a familial relationship of intimacy.

It's Not about You

Here's a paradox for you: while your Baptism is one of the most important events in your life, it is not essentially about you. The sacraments are not a self-improvement program or some way of creating a better version of yourself. Baptism, like all the sacraments, is about what God is doing in your life—namely, calling you to enter more deeply into God's world and to conform more closely to the image of his Son, Jesus Christ. Think about what happens when you make a new friend, someone you are completely enamored with. As you spend more time with this person, you find yourself picking up some of their mannerisms and habits (for better or worse). You may begin listening to the music they like, watching their favorite TV shows, eating their favorite foods, repeating their common phrases, or even making some of their typical facial expressions. Relationships form us and shape us into a new person. In Baptism, we are shaped into Christ himself.

> **In Baptism, we do not become a better version of ourselves; we become a version of Christ himself.**

Ultimately, Baptism reorients us, shifting our attention away from ourselves and toward the needs of others. Baptism initiates us into a way of life that is characterized by laying down one's life and setting aside one's own needs to pay attention to the needs of others. Baptism is not a cozy little "me-and-God" moment that cements our place in heaven but rather a "we-and-God" experience that thrusts us into the midst of a humanity in which God dwells. Baptism is manifested most powerfully in the acts of feeding the hungry, clothing the naked, visiting the sick and imprisoned, housing the homeless, and comforting the afflicted. It is not a magic ticket to heaven but rather an access code to living in an alternate reality, beginning right here and now, where God reigns and where God's selfless love is the new normal. In Baptism, we do not become a better version of ourselves; we become a version of Christ himself.

Water

As NASA continues to search the cosmos for the possibility of life on other planets, the search is always guided by detecting signs of water. Where there is water, there is life.

Strangely enough, though, where there is water, there is also death. In 2004, a quarter of a million people were killed by a horrific tsunami off the coast of Indonesia. Aside from natural disasters, every day in the United States an average of ten people die from unintentional drowning. Water kills. In Scripture, water's first appearance is equated with chaos. Water wipes out all living things except for Noah and his family and the animals he has saved aboard his ark. When the Jewish people fled Egypt, they were doing fine until they reached the Red Sea, which meant certain death for them. It was only through the intervention of God, through Moses, that the Israelites passed through the waters—passed through death—in order to continue their journey to the Promised Land.

It is no coincidence, then, that water is the primary symbol of Baptism. When we enter into the waters of Baptism, we are not only washed clean and refreshed, but we also die. As we burst forth from the waters and our lungs fill up with air, we are filled with new life. Sin affects us like water—it causes us to drown. Like the waters of the Red Sea, sin can only be overcome by an intervention from God: we cannot save ourselves. When we surrender control and allow God to enter into our lives, at first we sink. We die. However, God reaches down into the depths and pulls us out, breathing life into our lifeless body and spirit. Where there is water, there is life and death and life.

> **Like the waters of the Red Sea, sin can only be overcome by an intervention from God: we cannot save ourselves.**

Thin Moments: Water

Water is part of daily life, which means that you have numerous opportunities every day to recall and be thankful for your Baptism:

> - when you wake up each morning and take that first drink of water to quench your thirst and renew your parched throat
> - when you splash water on your face or step under the shower to wash away sleep
> - when you see or step into any body of water: a stream, river, lake, ocean, even a puddle
> - when you observe or get caught in a downpour of rain
> - when water is served to you at a restaurant

Oil

I grew up surrounded by pills, tablets, capsules, liniments, elixirs, tonics, syrups, salves, creams, ointments, tinctures, and oils. Such were the many remedies available at Paprocki Pharmacy, each one promising healing and restoration. Oils, in particular, served many functions:

+ restoring dried and damaged skin
+ relieving aches and pains
+ renewing and strengthening muscles
+ protecting against the elements
+ healing rashes and other skin maladies

Oils have always been viewed as possessing these helpful "powers," which explains the ancient practice of anointing. To anoint someone was to unleash upon and imbue them with powers beyond themselves. Scripture tells us that kings were anointed as a sign of divine power overcoming them. In Baptism, the anointing with oil symbolizes this very reality—the fact that the one being baptized is now overcome with a power beyond himself or herself, namely, the power of the Holy Spirit. Just as oils, creams, and liniments need more than one application to have the desired effect, the anointing we receive at Baptism is a ritual anointing that symbolizes the "daily anointing" we need to receive if we are to experience the full effect of the Holy Spirit. Every day of our lives, we pray for this holy anointing, which is nothing less than the pouring forth of the Holy Spirit into our lives—a power beyond ourselves, which, like the oil used to polish silver, reveals the luster of the image of God that we were created with.

Oil also has another important quality: it's messy. An oil spill in the home is a nuisance. An oil spill in the ocean is a disaster. Oil cannot be controlled; it gets all over the place and permeates everything it touches. It leaves an indelible stain. It oozes, drips, seeps, flows, and soaks. In the same way, the Holy Spirit is not under our control: to be anointed with oil is to invite an oil spill into our lives that unleashes a divine force that permeates the fabric of our being. This spiritual oil spill,

> The Holy Spirit is not under our control: to be anointed with oil is to invite an oil spill into our lives that unleashes a divine force that permeates the fabric of our being.

Thin Moments: Oil

You can use the following encounters with oil to recall and be thankful for the gift of anointing in Baptism:

> when you rub on any ointment, cream, or lotion to renew your skin or relieve pain
> when you pour oil into a frying pan
> when you use oil to lubricate a hinge on a door
> when you put on suntan lotion or oil
> when you fill up your car with gas or get an oil change

though not destructive, is overpowering: the Holy Spirit is not a cute little dove but a Person who gets under our skin and persistently fills our mind in a very compelling and indelible way. This is precisely why Pope Francis, when speaking to young people at World Youth Day in Brazil in 2015, told them to return to their dioceses and parishes and "make a mess!"

Fire

Like oil, fire has both good and bad qualities. Fire gives light, provides warmth, softens metals, and cooks our food. It also destroys and consumes. This is why we have been warned since we were children not to play with matches lest we burn ourselves and others or set the house on fire. And yet, we are attracted to fire: the smell of a campfire is invigorating, the dancing flames are hypnotic, and the crackling sounds are soothing. When left in the cold to battle the elements, we turn to fire to keep us alive.

It is no surprise, then, that Scripture often compares the divine presence to fire. God appeared to Moses in a burning bush. As the Jewish people set forth from Egypt on their desert journey, they were led by a pillar of fire at night and a column of smoke by day. When the Spirit descended upon the Apostles and Mary on Pentecost, we are told that tongues of fire appeared above their heads. The divine presence, like fire, is something we rely on but cannot control. The divine presence provides light for our eyes and warmth for our hearts. God gives us comfort and melts our hearts like wax so we can be shaped into the divine image. At the same time, we approach the divine presence cautiously knowing that God, like fire, must be met with eyes wide open and with an attitude of respect for that which is greater than ourselves. And yet, when all is said and done, at our Baptism, we are handed this fire via a candle and are told to "keep the flame of faith alive in your hearts." God trusts us not only to draw near to the fire of his love but to allow it to enter into us and transform us.

> God trusts us not only to draw near to the fire of his love but to allow it to enter into us and transform us.

White Garment

A few years back, the Chicago Blackhawks found themselves short a goalie in Philadelphia because their starter, Corey Crawford, had an emergency appendectomy just hours before game time. They quickly scoured the Philly area for a backup. That backup turned out to be Eric Semborski, a twenty-three-year-old who was coaching a kids' hockey league on behalf of the Philadelphia Flyers. The Hawks signed him to a one-game contract two hours before the game and put him through the motions of preparing for a professional hockey game. Semborski never did get to play in the game, and at the end of the day, his NHL career was over. However, several days later, he was invited to the United Center in Chicago and, as a sign of the team's appreciation, was presented with a goalie stick signed by the entire team, a goalie mask, and, most importantly, an official Chicago Blackhawks jersey with his name on it. The Hawks management told him, "Once you're a Blackhawk, you're always a Blackhawk. Even if it was just for one day."

Putting on a team jersey has profound symbolism in the world of sports. When a team acquires a new player and introduces him at a press conference, the climax of the introduction is the donning of the team jersey. The

Thin Moments: White Garment

When you choose your wardrobe every day and then put on your clothes or a uniform, call to mind the fact that in Baptism, you have put on Christ. Ask for the grace you need to put on Christ this day and every day. Do the same when you try on clothes at a department store or every time you change clothes throughout the day.

message is clear: you belong to an organization and, by donning this uniform, you are expected to live up to the values and standards of that organization whether you're physically wearing the uniform or not.

In Baptism, a similar gesture takes place: the presentation and donning of a white garment to symbolize putting on Christ. While a white garment is worn ritually only at Baptism and again in death (when the coffin of a Catholic is draped in white), each Christian is called to "put on Christ" every day so that we can truly project to others an image of God—the imago Dei—which is our true calling. As the words of the Rite of Baptism say: "You have become a new creation, and have clothed yourself in Christ. See in this white garment the outward sign of your Christian dignity. With your family and friends to help you by word and example, bring that dignity unstained into the everlasting life of heaven."

> **Each Christian is called to "put on Christ" every day so that we can truly project to others an image of God—the imago Dei—which is our true calling.**

Why Wait?

For many of us, Baptism occurred when we were infants. This does not mean that we missed it. Quite the contrary: this chapter has illustrated how each of us can and must renew our Baptism every day of our lives. So, why infant Baptism? Shouldn't we wait until a person is old enough to decide for himself or herself? The fact is, infant Baptism has a long tradition in the Church and has its basis in Scripture where we read that Lydia was baptized "with her household" (Acts 16:15) as was the Philippian jailer who was baptized "with all his family" (Acts 16:33). St. Paul also refers to baptizing "the household of Stephanas" (1 Corinthians 1:16).

Parents who want to give their children the greatest gift imaginable—salvation in Jesus Christ through the Church—are encouraged to bring their infants to Baptism as they commit themselves to bringing up their children in the Catholic faith, so that they may live out their Baptism and embrace it fully as they mature. There is no reason to wait if the family commits to helping their children recognize that Baptism wasn't an event that they missed but a gift they received that keeps on giving.

Living the Sacrament of Baptism

So, if we are called to reflect more closely the divine image in Baptism—the imago Dei—we need to reflect on what that means. When we look to Jesus Christ as the "face of God," we find that Jesus' life and ministry can be characterized in three words: priest, prophet, and king. Thus, in Baptism, we are called to share in these three roles of Christ: "God, the Father of our Lord Jesus Christ . . . now anoints you with the chrism of salvation. As Christ was anointed priest, prophet, and king, so may you live always as a member of his body, sharing everlasting life."

As disciples of Christ, we are called to love and serve God and others by sharing in Jesus' ministry as *priest*, *prophet*, and *king*. This means that we live the sacrament of Baptism by doing the following:

✚ **As priest:** Help others gain access to God.

✚ **As prophet:** Speak and act on behalf of the oppressed and fight for justice.

✚ **As king:** Serve and protect the vulnerable.

> "The rediscovery of the value of one's Baptism is the basis of the missionary commitment of every Christian."
> —Pope Benedict XVI

Scripture

Now there was a Pharisee, a man named Nicodemus who was a member of the Jewish ruling council. He came to Jesus at night and said, "Rabbi, we know that you are a teacher who has come from God. For no one could perform the signs you are doing if God were not with him." Jesus replied, "Very truly I tell you, no one can see the kingdom of God unless they are born again." "How can someone be born when they are old?" Nicodemus asked. "Surely they cannot enter a second time into their mother's womb to be born!" Jesus answered, "Very truly I tell you, no one can enter the kingdom of God unless they are born of water and the Spirit. Flesh gives birth to flesh, but the Spirit gives birth to spirit." (JOHN 3:1–6)

Prayer

Thank you, Lord, for the day of my liberation, the day of my Baptism. Thank you for changing my narrative from one of the mirage of self-sufficiency to one in which I can rely on you for rescue, restoration, and reassurance. Grant me the grace I need each day to overcome the dysfunction of sin. May my Baptism continue to color my world so that I recognize you and your grace in all things. Thank you for making me your adopted child through Baptism, which has elevated me from one of your creatures to one of your children. Waters of Baptism, wash over me daily. Oil of Baptism, get under my skin. Fire of Baptism, melt my heart. Garment of Baptism, clothe me in grace. Amen.

Chapter 3
Living the Sacrament of Confirmation: What's Come Over You?

Preparation for Confirmation should aim at leading the Christian toward a more intimate union with Christ and a livelier familiarity with the Holy Spirit–his actions, his gifts, and his biddings–in order to be more capable of assuming the apostolic responsibilities of Christian life. (*Catechism of the Catholic Church*, no. 1309)

What's Come Over You?

No doubt, you're familiar with the phrase "What's come over you?"—a question we ask someone (similar to asking "What's gotten into you?") when he or she appears to be affected by something. He or she might respond, "I was looking through old family pictures, and something came over me." We use the phrase to describe the reality that something outside ourselves can affect us within and transform the way we think, feel, speak, and act.

In the Gospels, people often wanted to know what had "come over" Jesus. When they witnessed some of the things Jesus said and did—things that no ordinary man would say or do—they asked variations of the question, "What's come over you?"

- "What is this?" (Mark 1:27)
- "Why does this fellow talk like that?" (Mark 2:7)
- "Why does he eat with tax collectors and sinners?" (Mark 2:16)
- "Who is this?" (Mark 4:41)
- "Where did this man get these things?" (Mark 6:2)
- "What's this wisdom that has been given him?" (Mark 6:2)

➕ "What are these remarkable miracles he is performing?" (Mark 6:2)

➕ "Isn't this the carpenter?" (Mark 6:3)

People who saw Jesus perform miracles and heard him teach with such authority concluded that he had a spirit that was beyond human, a spirit that could come only from God. They saw Jesus as the intersection of heaven and earth. This is why, when Jesus finally asked his Apostles, "Who do you say that I am?" Peter responded, "You are the Messiah" (Mark 8:29). This was Peter's way of asserting that Jesus was filled (anointed) with a spirit that comes only from God. The Jewish people believed that it was possible to receive something spiritual, not only from God but also from another person—something from outside themselves that could transform and renew them from within. They imagined this "something spiritual" as being "poured out" as one pours out a precious oil. Thus, they spoke of receiving the spirit of God as "being anointed" and they spoke of Jesus as "the Christ," which means "the anointed one."

> People who saw Jesus perform miracles and heard him teach with such authority concluded that he had a spirit that was beyond human, a spirit that could come only from God.

Before long, followers of the Christ concluded that by learning about him, they could share in his spirit. Likewise, they soon came to recognize that the same Spirit that filled Jesus could be "transferred" from one person to another through the act of anointing with oil and laying on of hands. On the Feast of Pentecost, when the Apostles were filled with the Holy Spirit and went into the streets preaching about the risen Christ, people reacted by asking, for all intents and purposes, "What's come over them?" In fact, Scripture tells us that people concluded that the Apostles were drunk because nothing else could explain the transformation that had "come over them" (Acts 2:13).

COME, FOLLOW ME.

UM... TELL ME ABOUT THE BENEFITS. IS THERE A GOOD RETIREMENT PLAN? DENTAL? WHAT ABOUT A 401 K?

At the heart of being filled with the Spirit is the notion of experiencing a transformation. It was a change of behavior for the better that the Apostles considered evidence that a person had been filled with the Holy Spirit because he or she no longer seemed to be living by the power of an ordinary human spirit. Those whose lives had been transformed by living according to the spirit of Jesus Christ were referred to as having been "anointed." It is precisely this transformation—from ordinary people into disciples of Jesus—that is at the heart of all the sacraments. In the Sacrament of Confirmation, we celebrate the transformation that takes place when heaven and earth intersect in the hearts of those who are filled with the Holy Spirit.

Be Careful What You Ask For

My friend Vickie Tufano tells a story (which she attributes to her friend William Willimon, a professor at Duke University) of a campus minister who received a phone call from an irate parent who was calling to complain that his daughter had chosen to ignore her degree in engineering in favor of becoming a missionary. He blamed the campus minister for filling his daughter's head with all kinds of radical ideas and "religion stuff." The campus minister replied by asking, "Weren't you the one who had her baptized?" "Well, yes," he said. "And then, didn't you read her Bible stories, take her to church on Sundays, let her go with the youth group to work in Appalachia?" "Well, yes, but . . . " "Don't 'but' me," the minister said. "It's your fault that she believed all that stuff, and that she's gone and 'thrown it all away' on Jesus, not mine. You're the one who introduced her to Jesus, not me." "But all we ever wanted was for her to be a good Catholic," the father said, meekly. The campus minister replied, "Sorry. I guess you've messed up; you made her a disciple."

In Baptism, we (or our parents) are invited to state what it is we are asking of the Church. When we ask for Baptism, we are asking for much more than a cultural identity or loose affiliation with an institution with a noble cause. We are asking to become disciples of Jesus Christ.

Be careful what you ask for!

Perhaps you've not thought of yourself as a disciple of Christ but only as a member of his Church. One can be a member of the Church without living a life of discipleship. The Sacrament of Confirmation invites us to revisit this baptismal commitment to discipleship and to invite God to strengthen it through the power of the Holy Spirit. To be a disciple of Jesus is to choose a new narrative and an alternate way of living—one in which God reigns. It is a life marked by selfless love. It is a life marked by joy and hope—a confidence that, in God, all shall be well.

> To be a disciple of Jesus is to choose a new narrative and an alternate way of living—one in which God reigns.

Dipped and Poured

If you're a chocolate lover, imagine a friend telling you about a place where you can get the best chocolate dessert imaginable. "They have so much chocolate that I bet they not only dip their dessert in chocolate but then they pour chocolate all over it!" Sound extravagant? Dipping and pouring seems to be way over the top. And yet, as the first Christians sought to express the "deep down things" that happen to people when they become followers of Jesus Christ, they described it using similarly extravagant metaphors—namely, Baptism and Confirmation.

The word *Baptism* literally means to "dip," "dunk," "plunge," or, to be more sophisticated, to "immerse" for the purpose of saturating or, better yet, marinating—a process in which one substance deeply penetrates another. In Baptism, we are immersed in Christ—dipped, dunked, and plunged into the waters of Christ's Death and Resurrection to be saturated or marinated in the deeply penetrating spirit of Jesus. As if that weren't enough, however, the first Christians poured it on (literally) by insisting that when one is immersed into Jesus Christ, his Spirit pours over you. In Confirmation, the same Spirit into whom we have been dipped in Baptism now pours over us. The message is simple, clear, and powerful: as long as we continue to immerse ourselves in Jesus Christ—to live our Baptism—his Spirit will continue to pour over us, enabling us to live our Confirmation.

> "Those in whom the Spirit comes to live are God's new Temple. They are, individually and corporately, places where heaven and earth meet."
> —N. T. WRIGHT, *SIMPLY CHRISTIAN: WHY CHRISTIANITY MAKES SENSE*

Roots and Wings

While Baptism and Confirmation are two distinct sacraments, they are intimately linked and work together to transform us. While Baptism invites us to participate in the Paschal Mystery (Jesus' Death and Resurrection), Confirmation invites us to participate in the completion of the Paschal Mystery (the reception of the Holy Spirit). While Baptism gives us roots, Confirmation gives us wings. While Baptism grounds us in the reality of Jesus Christ, Confirmation calls us to soar on the wings of the Spirit. While Baptism awakens us to the immanence of God and his participation in our lives, Confirmation awakens us to the transcendence of God and our participation in the divine life. While Baptism calls us to do soul work (pay attention to our innermost reality), Confirmation compels us to do spirit work (pay attention to our connection to the supernatural).

Having said the above, however, we must be careful to avoid imagining a sharp distinction between soul and spirit; the two are complementary and intimately woven together. When looking at Baptism and Confirmation in this manner, it is clear that they are inseparable. In the early Church, they were seen as two distinct movements and actions within the same seamless reality of Christian initiation. It wasn't until the Church began to grow rapidly after Constantine's Edict of Milan in the early fourth century and bishops found it impossible to be present at each and every Baptism that Confirmation was separated from Baptism.

As a result, for too many of us, our experiences of Baptism and Confirmation are like being the child of divorced parents who rarely interact with one another. In this unfortunate metaphor, Baptism assumes the role of our birth mother—the one directly responsible for bringing us into this world—while Confirmation is too often relegated to the role of a distant father whose contribution to our life pales in comparison. This isn't true, however, if you understand the intimate connection between Baptism and Confirmation.

"You Can't Have Him"

On the rare occasions when a woman at some social gathering saw fit to flirt with me, the maneuver never escaped my wife's radar. Within seconds, my bride would assertively take her place at my side and entwine her arm around mine and say to the woman, "You can't have him" before leading me away. The message was unmistakably clear: "He's mine. He belongs to me."

In Baptism and Confirmation, we embrace a narrative in which God essentially says to those other realities that temptingly whisper promises of happiness in our ears, "You can't have him/her. He/she belongs to me." In Baptism, we are sealed with the Sign of the Cross. In Confirmation, we are sealed with the anointing. In both actions, we are claimed by Christ and are lovingly warned, "Don't get any ideas." Just as my wife reminds me that no one could ever love me as she does (I'm one lucky guy!), the sacraments remind us that no one could ever love us as God loves us and that no one or nothing could bring the fulfillment that God's love brings us. Here, I paraphrase my friend, author and liturgist D. Todd Williamson, who once preached similar words at a prayer service: "Once you're claimed by Christ, it means that nothing else can have you. Sickness can't have you. Anxiety can't have you. Depression can't have you. Temptation can't have you. Sadness can't have you. Material possessions can't have you. No, not even death can have you!" Being claimed by Christ does not prevent these things from occurring but asserts that none of them can have the final say.

> **In Baptism and Confirmation, God essentially says to those other realities that temptingly whisper promises of happiness in our ears, "You can't have him/her. He/she belongs to me."**

Anointed Means Appointed

When a leader chooses, selects, or appoints a successor, we might say that he or she has "anointed" a successor. When assuming leadership, it helps to have the blessing of your predecessor and/or other significant people. This notion of anointing someone to assume a leadership role has deep roots in Scripture and history. In the Old Testament, we learn that priests and kings were anointed with oil as a visible sign of being commissioned or appointed. The gesture of anointing was intended to show that what was being received by the new leader was coming from God; the person receiving the anointing was standing at the intersection of heaven and earth, imbued with divine grace and under God's protection. Anyone "messing" with God's anointed one was "messing" with God.

> **Anyone "messing" with God's anointed one was "messing" with God.**

Oil: Nature's Petri Dish

While we know that life emerged from water, scientists now tell us that the life that formed in water needed protection from external forces and turbulence while keeping essential ingredients and allowing waste and toxins to flow out. This protection took the form of oily membranes, nature's petri dish or "vessel" for life.

While water and oil do not mix, they can cooperate. In the same way, the waters of Baptism and the oils of Confirmation cooperate: the waters give life and the oil protects it from the dangers of sin that seek to creep in and disrupt the life that God offers us.

You're Gonna Go Places!

People join organizations for a variety of reasons. One of them is the hope that membership will enable you to "go places"—a phrase we use to refer to someone who is reaching his or her dreams.

Similarly, the purpose of Baptism is not to become a member of a group so that you can hang around with other Christians. We join the Church because we believe it will help us "go places"—namely, into the presence of God, both in this world and in eternity. Confirmation celebrates this

Once upon a time, a bishop was celebrating a Confirmation at a parish and, in speaking with the confirmands, encouraged them to go beyond their comfort zones and perhaps even visit the Holy Land someday. The following summer, the bishop himself went on a pilgrimage to the Holy Land and decided to go for a boat tour on the Sea of Galilee. When he got in the boat, he recognized the boatman as one of the confirmands, who, it turns out, not only had visited the Holy Land but discovered that his family had roots in the boating industry going back to the time of Christ. The young man took the bishop on an incredible tour of the Sea of Galilee and afterward told the bishop his fee was five hundred dollars. When the bishop protested, the young man said, "That fee is commensurate with what my family has been charging for over two thousand years!" To which the bishop replied, "Well, at least now I have a better understanding of why Jesus chose to walk on water!"

aspect of our initiation: the outward focus of discipleship. The most palpable manifestation of a life truly immersed in Jesus Christ is a new narrative characterized by the shifting of one's attention from one's own needs to the needs of others. Compelled by the Spirit, disciples of Christ venture beyond their comfort zones to accompany others on the journey.

Living on Borrowed Breath

We have a strange phrase that we use when someone "cheats death" and bounces back to good health. We say that he or she is "living on borrowed time." By that saying, we imply that we live on time that belongs to us. In reality, however, we are living on borrowed time from the moment of our conception; we are stewards of the time God has given us on this planet.

When it comes to understanding our relationship with the Holy Spirit in the Sacrament of Confirmation, I suggest that we paraphrase the phrase "living on borrowed time" and recognize that each of us is living on "borrowed breath"—the very breath of God. Too often, the Holy Spirit seems to us to be an impersonal reality, a nebulous vapor swirling around us. Yet our faith teaches us that the Holy Spirit is a Person, one of the Three Persons of the Trinity. We know from our lived experience that to experience someone else's breath, we must be in close proximity to him or her (thus the need for brushing teeth and using mouthwash!).

When my wife and I visited Hawaii some years ago, our friend Jayne Mondoy took us sightseeing. At one scenic vista, we came across a family in traditional Hawaiian celebratory clothing, having just celebrated a wedding. The elderly parents greeted us very warmly and made a move to hug us, but, at the last second, surprised us by leaning in so that their foreheads and noses touched our foreheads and noses. It was quite moving and beautiful. Later, Jayne explained that this is the traditional Hawaiian greeting in which people share *ha*, or breath, by entering one another's "space" and inhaling, thus sharing the breath of life. The understanding is that for the meeting of two people to be a true encounter, they must exchange breath.

> **"Always be busy in spiritual actions. In this way, no matter how often the enemy of our souls approaches, he'll find our hearts closed and armed against him."**
> —St. Cyprian of Carthage

Thin Moments: Confirmation

The following everyday experiences can serve as opportunities for you to reflect on living the Sacrament of Confirmation:

> when you feel the wind blow or see a fan blowing something
> when you see a candle burning or light a match
> when you brush up against someone or someone brushes up against you
> when you pour something rich like syrup or honey
> when you see a bird take wing
> when you place a hand on someone's shoulder for reassurance
> when your hands are oily from applying a cream, lotion, or ointment
> when you get assigned/appointed to a new task or responsibility
> when you get an oil change for your car
> when you oil the hinges on a door

To help us overcome the notion that the Holy Spirit is an impersonal reality like the Force from *Star Wars*, all you need to do is to pause and take a deep breath, recognizing that you are living on borrowed breath—divine breath. When Jesus told the Apostles to receive the Holy Spirit, we are told that he breathed on them, a sign that he was sharing his divine life with them. That same Spirit, the same breath of God that hovered over creation at the beginning of time, dwells within each of us. This is why many prayer methods involve some type of conscious breathing: not only is it a way to slow down our metabolism, but it is also a way for us to encounter the divine presence within us.

We are all living on borrowed breath, an image that makes me think of my friend Pat who, after waiting three years, finally received a donor heart and underwent a successful heart transplant. Each day thereafter has been like a gift to him as he awakens daily to the realization that he is alive because of a "borrowed" heart. And, in a mysterious way, he will forever be in a profound relationship with that person who, in death, gave life to Pat by being an organ donor. In Confirmation, we are reminded that, like Pat, our very existence is dependent on the intervention of another Person whose breath fills our lungs daily.

We may exchange breath with people haphazardly such as when standing close to someone on a crowded bus or train. However, when we exchange breath with someone on a regular basis—when we are regularly in close proximity with someone—that intimacy enables us to get to know that person on a deeper level. As a result, when someone asks, "What is he/she really like?" we are able to share our experience of that person: "He/she is gentle, thoughtful, humorous, understanding, passionate," and so on. Our proximity to the Holy Spirit reveals that the Spirit is a Person who is wise, understanding, supportive, courageous, knowledgeable, profound, humble, loving, joyful, comforting, peaceful, patient, kind, good, faithful, gentle, inspiring, and renewing, just to name a few of the Spirit's divine qualities. When we are close to another person, it is common for him or her to rub off on us, something that the Holy Spirit has a knack for doing.

Anointing: May the Spirit "Rub Off on Us"

When talking about concepts such as anointing, we tend to jump immediately to the spiritual/religious understanding of the word, often overlooking its ordinary meaning, which means to pour, smear, or rub oil on someone or something. Long before anointing became a ritual act, it was an action of ordinary life, especially in dry Middle Eastern climates where anointing

The Laying On of Hands

Children innately understand that power can be transferred by touch, which is why they play games such as "It" or "Tag" in which the person who is "it" chases the other players in hopes of touching them—tagging them—and shouting "You're it!" thus transferring the essence of being "it" to that person. Throughout Scripture, touch is used to transfer power and authority from one person to another, such as when Moses laid hands on Joshua to appoint him as successor or when Jesus laid hands on those who were sick to transfer his healing power to them. In the Rite of Confirmation, the bishop and priests symbolically lay hands (by holding their outstretched arms over the group) on those being confirmed to symbolize the transferring of the Holy Spirit to them. This same gesture is used in the Sacraments of the Anointing of the Sick and Holy Orders.

When the Spirit Rubs Off on Us

St. Paul tells us that when the Holy Spirit "rubs off" on us, we take on the following qualities (Galatians 5:22–23):

> love (putting one's own needs aside to tend to the needs of others)
> joy (having lightness of being and the ability to brighten up a room)
> peace (living in a state of serenity, even when in turmoil)
> forbearance (winking at the foibles and shortcomings of others instead of putting people in their place)
> kindness (responding to even the grumpiest of people with graciousness and civility)
> goodness (keeping the best interests of others in mind, even when they fail us)
> faithfulness (staying on message, even under duress)
> gentleness (remaining even-keeled and reasonable in the face of conflict)
> self-control (practicing mindfulness)

was needed to moisturize one's skin. Anointing also had therapeutic and healing qualities. When one anointed another person with oil, the goal was to effect a change in that person, bringing dry skin to life, easing soreness and pain, increasing ease of motion, and restoring health where there was sickness.

As with bathing in water, this natural act of anointing with oil took on ritual meaning, symbolizing a transformation taking place on the spiritual level within a person. The key, however, is that the transformation is not an act of self-achievement but is rather attributed to the inspiration and power of a reality beyond oneself, namely divine power: the Holy Spirit of God. Just as we do not baptize ourselves or give ourselves the Eucharist, we do not anoint ourselves; we are anointed. In essence, the Holy Spirit "rubs off on us."

Think about that phrase for a moment. Through science, we know that each time we brush against something or wash ourselves, we rub off a top layer of skin that is replaced by a new layer. We use the phrase "rubs off on us" to describe the effect that occurs when we brush against or have a close association with another person and we begin to incorporate aspects or habits of that person, whether good or bad. When we are around upbeat, energetic people, we often remark that we wish some of their optimism and energy would rub off on us. When a child starts to pick up bad habits, we sometimes say that someone who is a bad influence is "rubbing off" on him or her.

Once anointed with the Holy Spirit, we are "oily," which means that when we brush up against others, we hope to rub off on them (and not rub them the wrong way!) to spread the qualities of the Holy Spirit throughout the world.

The Multivalent Symbolism of Anointing

Like water and fire, oil and the anointing with oil have many layers of meaning and symbolism. Here are a few more in addition to those addressed above:

✚ A person who is anointed no longer acts in his or her own capacity but is an envoy of the one who does the anointing. Like an ambassador sent to speak on behalf of a country's leader, we present our credentials—our anointing—to the world and work on God's behalf to achieve his purposes for his creation. The anointing also reminds us to whom we are responsible.

✚ When one is anointed, he or she is set apart or consecrated for a specific purpose. The act of anointing confers outwardly the authority that God has placed on the anointed to act and speak on his behalf.

✚ When applied to skin, oil permeates, saturates, penetrates, and lingers. The anointing with oil symbolizes the ways in which the Holy Spirit permeates our being, saturates us with grace, penetrates our hearts, and produces a lingering effect that is noticeable to others.

✚ In biblical times, oil was, unlike water, in abundance; it was found in most every household for cooking purposes, for light and heat, for cosmetic purposes, and for therapeutic/medicinal purposes. Oil was everywhere, especially when spilled.

> The anointing with oil symbolizes the ways in which the Holy Spirit permeates our being, saturates us with grace, penetrates our hearts, and produces a lingering effect that is noticeable to others.

Olive oil, which was the most common, could be found everywhere. Anointing with sacred Chrism made from olive oil symbolizes the abundance (and ordinariness) of God's grace, which is everywhere and can be found in all things. And, like oil spilled, it cannot be contained.

✚ To anoint someone was to choose them, appoint them, consecrate them, and equip them for their mission. Through our anointing in Confirmation, we are reminded that God has chosen us, has appointed us to carry out his mission, has consecrated us (set us apart for God's purposes), and continually equips us if we seek the Spirit's help, guidance, and support.

✚ When oil is applied to the skin, it makes the skin glisten or glow. It renews that which is dried and cracked. The anointing we receive from the Holy Spirit calls us to radiate God's grace—to be a light to others—and to renew that which is broken in ourselves, in others, and in our world.

✚ In everyday living, anointing with oil seeks to bring about a new reality within an existing one: moist skin in a dry environment; healing where there is sickness; strength where there is weakness; light where there is darkness; warmth where there is cold and flavor where there is blandness. In Confirmation, the anointing with oil signifies bringing about a new reality in our lives and in the lives of others, seeking to bring about the kind of transformation we hear of in the Prayer of St. Francis:

Where there is hatred let me sow love;
Where there is injury, pardon;
Where there is doubt, faith;
Where there is despair, hope;
Where there is darkness, light;
And where there is sadness, joy.

✚ Ancient wrestlers applied oil to their bodies to make it difficult for their opponent to grab hold of them. St. Ambrose famously taught that the anointing with oil achieves the same purpose, making it more difficult for the enemy—Satan—to grab hold of us. This is one situation in which it is complimentary to be thought of as "slippery"!

- We use the phrase "grease the skids" to refer to the act of making preparations that will allow subsequent activities to be achieved more easily. To literally "grease the skids" is to oil the pallets over which something will be dragged to reach another destination. The anointing in Confirmation paves the way or "greases the skids" to move us easily from the first Sacrament of Initiation–Baptism–to the sacrament that completes our initiation: the Eucharist.

- Because oil was abundant in biblical times, it easily became a symbol of generosity and joy. Jesuit priest, paleontologist, and philosopher, Pierre Teilhard de Chardin, borrowing from the French writer Léon Bloy, referred to joy as the most infallible sign of the presence of God. It makes sense, then, that oil is poured, rubbed, smeared generously in the anointing at Confirmation to express outwardly the joy that comes with being filled with the Spirit of God.

- Anointing with oil was seen as a vehicle for transporting powerful qualities and attributes from the external world to the internal world. Oil had qualities not found within ourselves. Thus, to be anointed was to be "overtaken" by a reality beyond oneself. The Gospels speak of Mary being "overshadowed" by the Holy Spirit (Luke 1:35), meaning that what was about to happen to her–giving birth to a son–would be the result of a power beyond herself. When we are anointed with oil, we are reminded that we are being overshadowed by the Holy Spirit, by a power, a force, a Person more powerful than ourselves and capable of bringing about significant change within us.

> **Anointing with oil was seen as a vehicle for transporting powerful qualities and attributes from the external world to the internal world.**

The Holy Spirit Is a Person, Not a Vapor

At the heart of the Sacrament of Confirmation is the reality of being sealed with the Holy Spirit. Too often, we think of the Holy Spirit as an impersonal entity. The Holy Spirit, however, is not a vapor or a vague, amorphous reality. The Holy Spirit is a Person, someone with whom we are called to have a relationship. While Scripture uses symbols such as wind, fire, and a dove to describe the Holy Spirit, Jesus refers to the Holy Spirit as our advocate. An advocate is a person who stands by your side defending you, promoting you, accompanying you, supporting you, and pleading on your behalf.

When I was once teaching eighth graders about the Holy Spirit as an advocate, I was blessed to have as my catechist's aide a nurse from Advocate Christ Hospital. I invited her—let's call her Mrs. Columba, Latin for "dove"—to describe how, as a nurse, she advocated for patients and for the newborn infants in the maternity ward where she served. She did a marvelous job of explaining how she helped patients overcome their fear, find strength and trust, and be courageous. She explained how she would speak up for her patients, asking doctors to respond to their specific needs. When she was done, I told the young people, "When the bishop confirms you and tells you that you are sealed with the Holy Spirit, think of Mrs. Columba and you'll have a good idea of who is your Advocate!"

St. Cyril of Jerusalem referred to the Holy Spirit as "the friend closest to our hearts," one who "comes with the tenderness of a true friend and protector to save, to heal, to teach, to counsel, to strengthen, to console." These are things a vapor or a nebulous force cannot do. The Person of the Holy Spirit is a powerful person, someone capable of bringing about change within us. Acts of the Apostles tells us that when the early Christians gathered in prayer, "the place where they were meeting was shaken" (Acts 4:31). In other words, the Holy Spirit possesses the capability of shaking us up. Think for a moment of people in your life who shook you up, for better or for worse. We talk about "falling head over heels for someone," which is most definitely an image of being shaken up. We talk about being "thrown for a loop" by someone, meaning that they shook us up. When we enter a relationship with the Holy Spirit, we will be shaken up. Is it possible that when you pray, the place where you pray will be shaken? Yes, but only if you understand that it means that you yourself are being shaken by your relationship with the Holy Spirit.

While we have many beautiful prayers to the Holy Spirit, I would suggest one more: "Come, Holy Spirit, and shake me up!"

> While we have many beautiful prayers to the Holy Spirit, I would suggest one more: "Come, Holy Spirit, and shake me up!"

Scripture

You have loved righteousness and hated wickedness; therefore God, your God, has set you above your companions by anointing you with the oil of joy. (HEBREWS 1:9)

Prayer

Come, Holy Spirit, and shake me up! Transform my heart so that it more closely resembles the heart of Jesus. Rub off on me so that I might, in turn, transfer your qualities of love, joy, peace, forbearance, kindness, goodness, faithfulness, gentleness, and self-control to others. Equip me, appoint me, and overtake me. Anoint me each day so that I will live under God's protection, and may I be saturated with grace. Pour over me in a messy fashion to remind me that I am not in control, and make me "slippery" so that the enemy cannot grab hold of me. Amen.

Chapter 4
Living the Sacrament of the Eucharist: What Do You Crave?

In brief, the Eucharist is the sum and summary of our faith: "Our way of thinking is attuned to the Eucharist, and the Eucharist in turn confirms our way of thinking." (*Catechism of the Catholic Church*, no. 1327)

What Do You Crave?

Researchers tell us that the majority of us experience regular cravings for specific foods. My wife, for example, regularly craves something sweet. To her credit, she is a "sweets snob" and will not settle for *anything* sweet but only something that meets her high standards. Unfortunately, many of us satisfy our cravings by settling for less than the best.

> **Hunger seeks to satisfy a physical need; a craving seeks to satisfy an emotional one.**

It's important to remember that hunger and cravings are not synonymous. The former is driven by the body, while the latter is driven by the mind. Hunger seeks to satisfy a physical need; a craving seeks to satisfy an emotional one. That's why cravings are not limited to food. We can find ourselves craving any and all of the following:

- a drink
- sleep
- sex
- power
- possessions
- friendship
- novelty
- intimacy
- contentment
- fun
- pleasure
- adventure

The list can go on. The bottom line is that cravings seek to fulfill a sense of incompleteness. While hunger is utilitarian (for survival), cravings are for satisfaction: to fill a fundamental lack, flaw, or sense of inadequacy. Certain cues trigger our emotional response, which heightens our desire. Chemicals in the brain, such as dopamine, are released and narrow our focus to the one thing that we believe will satisfy us. In the end, we find ourselves desiring the following three fundamental things:

+ We crave something **substantial** so that it **fulfills** us. If we crave something sweet, we prefer something substantial like a piece of fudge rather than a cheap candy bar.

+ We crave something **delightful** so that it **pleases** us. Whether it is food, drink, or a piece of art, we gravitate toward those things that look, smell, taste, and feel pleasing.

+ We crave something **valuable** so that it **benefits** us. It often seems as though we crave things that are just beyond our usual reach, either physically or financially.

We hope that, by possessing these three things, we will successfully transcend our present narrative of incompleteness to one of fulfillment, even if temporary. This brings us to the Sacrament of the Eucharist, the "food" that promises to satisfy our deepest cravings. St. Ignatius of Loyola taught that, ultimately, all our desires can be traced to our desire for God. The *Catechism of the Catholic Church* teaches us that "the desire for God is written in the human heart" (no. 27). Our deepest craving is for a fulfillment that only God can provide. God, in turn, continually goes out of his way to provide us with access to the food that is his grace, culminating in the sending of his only Son, Jesus, who was born in Bethlehem—a name that means "house of bread"—and laid in a manger, which is a feeding trough for animals. Jesus referred to himself as the Bread of Life and, in his final act before giving himself up to be sacrificed like a lamb, he gave us the Eucharist: his presence in the form of simple bread and wine.

Our deepest craving is for a fulfillment that only God can provide.

Why, Then, Do We Continue to Eat Junk Food?

I can have a basket of fresh fruit sitting nearby in the kitchen and still find myself rummaging through the cabinets for a snack to satisfy my cravings. Even when we know what is best for us, our cravings often drive us to seek alternatives. This brings us to the story of Adam and Eve! Convinced by the serpent that their lives were incomplete, they sought to possess (and consume) something that would enable them to transcend their present narrative and enjoy a new narrative that promised a heightened state ("you will be like gods," Genesis 3:5). Adam and Eve craved something that was

- ➕ substantial ("the tree was good for food")
- ➕ delightful ("pleasing to the eyes")
- ➕ valuable ("desirable for gaining wisdom")

Adam and Eve—who represent all of human-kind—sought truth, beauty, and goodness: three things known traditionally as the transcendentals because they are considered attributes of God who embodies them. We crave truth, beauty, and goodness because we are made in the image and likeness of God. The only problem is, like Adam and Eve we continually seek these three things in the wrong places. Adam and Eve ate of the tree from which God specifically told them not to eat: they ate the wrong thing. God's only Son, Jesus Christ, came to show us the right thing to eat: the Bread of Life.

> **We crave truth, beauty, and goodness because we are made in the image and likeness of God. The only problem is, like Adam and Eve we continually seek these three things in the wrong places.**

Jesus' Cravings

Jesus dealt with human cravings and was tempted during his forty days in the desert to find truth, beauty, and goodness in something other than God. Unlike Adam and Eve, however, Jesus overcame these temptations and invites and empowers us to do the same. The chart on the following page illustrates what we crave, how Adam and Eve sought to fill those cravings in the "forbidden fruit," how Jesus was tempted to do the same, and what Jesus chose instead.

We Crave These Transcendentals:	TRUTH	BEAUTY	GOODNESS
This Transcendental Relates to the	mind	soul	heart
This Transcendental Affects How We	think	wish	feel/act
This Transcendental Achieves the Above by Providing	substance that fulfills us and gives us a reason to live	delight that pleases us and gives us a desire to live	value that benefits us and gives us a way to live
The "Apple" of Adam and Eve Was	substantial—it was "good for food"	delightful—it was "pleasing to the eyes"	valuable "for gaining wisdom"
Jesus' Temptations Were	to find sustenance by turning stone to bread	to delight in a flashy show in which God's angels save him	to find value in all the kingdoms of the world
Jesus Instead Chose	to be sustained by every word that comes from the mouth of God	to delight in God instead of putting him to the test	to find value in worshiping and serving God alone

Unlike other animals in God's creation, we human beings desire to transcend ourselves, to be transported beyond the merely physical and material to an experience of the spiritual. Unlike other creatures in God's creation, we are also capable of changing our narrative. We crave an encounter with mystery—to touch "deep down things," as the poet Gerard Manley Hopkins put it—and, in turn, to be touched by mystery. Jesus shows us that such cravings are not wrong but that how we choose to satisfy them often is.

Desire Is Not Wrong

One thing Christianity often got wrong over the centuries was the place of desire in the spiritual life. Specifically, we have sought to repress desire based on a misunderstanding of St. Paul's advice to the Romans (13:14) in which he says to "make no provision for the flesh, to gratify its desires." For St. Paul, "life in the flesh" is life that is mindless, rooted in patterns of behavior that our naturally self-centered brain dictates, what Buddhist monk Thich Nhat Hanh refers to as "machine thinking" or thinking like the person "who lives as though dead" (*The Miracle of Mindfulness*). "Life in the Spirit," on the other hand, requires a mindfulness that shifts the focus away from the self and toward others. In his *Spiritual Exercises*, St. Ignatius speaks not of repressing our desires but of "ordering" or redirecting them to God. For Catholics, to receive the Eucharist weekly is to order our desires: to live mindfully, acknowledging that it is God alone who fulfills our deepest desires.

Through the Eucharist, we cultivate an *awareness and integration* of our desires and imperfections, not the removal of them. The various negative behaviors that we engage in, seeking temporary relief from our cravings, ultimately dull our awareness. A life that is nourished by the Eucharist is a life focused on being awake and mindful, not about being asleep and mindless. It is about paying attention to our cravings. Author John Eldredge tells us as much in his book, *The Journey of Desire* (Nelson Publishing, 2000, p. 182) when he says that we basically face three choices when it comes to our desires:

1. We can be dead (in total denial of our desires).
2. We can be addicted (engaging in behaviors that make us comfortably numb).
3. We can be alive and thirsty.

He says that "to live in thirst is to live with an ache. Every addiction comes from the attempt to get rid of the ache."

We are invited to celebrate the Eucharist as an acknowledgment of our insatiable craving and a commitment to seek satisfaction of that craving in Jesus Christ, the Bread of Life. As St. Augustine said, "Our hearts are restless, Lord, until they find rest in you." The key is in how we attempt to satisfy our cravings. Is it any wonder, then, that Jesus offered his followers a meal as the key spiritual practice leading to satisfaction of their cravings? It is in this meal—the Eucharist—that Catholics find true

> **"Our hearts are restless, Lord, until they find rest in you."**
> —St. Augustine

nourishment and satisfaction for the hunger we all carry within. It is no accident, either, that this meal involves not only food but also alcohol! Jesus takes the very things that can be so easily abused and transforms them into that which can transform us, namely, his very self.

That's what the Eucharist is all about. From the moment we enter the church for Mass, we are being invited and challenged to realize that God alone sustains us. Throughout the rest of the week, we are subtly seduced by a different narrative that tells us something else can sustain us. Little by little, we can fall prey to the illusion that we will find happiness if we buy certain clothes, drive a certain car, maintain a certain weight, have a certain body shape, live in a certain area or type of home, have a certain kind of job, make a certain salary, have a certain amount of sex, achieve a certain level of popularity, and wield a certain amount of power.

> **From the moment we enter the church for Mass, we are being invited and challenged to realize that God alone sustains us.**

The narrative of the Eucharist is very clear: at our deepest level, we are incapable of sustaining ourselves. Every Sunday, when we receive Communion, we are reminded that although there's nothing inherently wrong with many of the things mentioned above, when we trust any of them to satisfy and sustain us, we have separated ourselves from our true source: the God who rescues us, restores us, and reassures us.

The Eucharist: The Ultimate Meal

In biblical times, sharing a meal with someone carried a more critical meaning than it does today. Because of the relative scarcity of food, to

After First Holy Communion practice, the children were invited into the parish hall for some snacks. At the head of the table was a large pile of apples. The director of religious education had posted the following note next to the apple tray: "Take only ONE. God is watching." Further along, one of the First Communicants spotted a large pile of chocolate chip cookies and quickly posted the following note: "Take all you want. God is watching the apples."

Thin Moments: Bread

Even if you are avoiding carbs, you still have many opportunities to reflect on the relationship between ordinary table bread/meals and the sustaining power of the Eucharist:

> when you go to a restaurant and bread is placed on the table
> when you smell fresh bread being baked
> when your stomach growls in hunger
> when you say grace before a meal
> when you bite into something delightful
> when you prepare a meal for someone else, especially those in need

share a meal with another person was to literally save their life for another day; it was an act of bonding and an expression of kinship and intimacy. For people of biblical times, the most essential food needed for survival was bread, referred to as the "staff of life" (Sirach 29:21), or that which helps one to walk.

Even today, bread is often brought to the table for free at restaurants, as a symbol of hospitality and a harbinger of more good things to come. Bread represents all food. It is also the perfect example of divine/human cooperation. While bread is created by human hands kneading and baking the dough, the dough is made possible by God, who provides the grain. It is no accident that Jesus chose bread as the medium for making himself available to us.

When the Church teaches us that the Eucharist is the "source and summit" of our lives (*Catechism of the Catholic Church*, no. 1324), it reminds us that God alone, who is present in the Eucharist, is our source of fulfillment. For Catholics, receiving Communion is the ultimate acknowledgment that God is our source.

When we come to recognize that God alone can satisfy our hunger and thirst, our lives find balance. We come to recognize that our craving, or, as Ronald Rolheiser refers to it, this "holy longing" (*The Holy Longing*, Doubleday, 1999), is ultimately a desire for God. This same recognition leads us to overcome the temptation to allow anything else to usurp God's role as the source of our satisfaction.

Living in a consumerist society, we may be tempted to treat the Eucharist as though it is a product and we are consumers. Naturally, like all consumers, we would expect immediate gratification. The Eucharist, however, is not a product. It's an embrace—not a momentary embrace but a lifelong one. Through our reception of the Eucharist, we are embraced by God, who heals and satisfies our craving.

At the same time, our reception of the Eucharist is an embrace not only of God but of our neighbors as well. The Eucharist is not a "me and God" experience. To share a table is to enter relationship with others. Likewise, we don't normally drink from the same cup that someone else is drinking from unless we have an intimate relationship with that person. So, we are, in a sense, becoming intimate with those who share the cup of Communion. Our communion with God is thus fulfilled by loving our brothers and sisters.

> **Through our reception of the Eucharist, we are embraced by God, who heals and satisfies our craving.**

Communion compels us to recognize the presence of God not only in the bread and wine but also in the flesh of those we encounter every day. Our worship of God, through the celebration of the Eucharist, is meaningless unless it points us in the direction of our neighbors.

"It's Just Lunch"

One of the top online matchmaking and dating services is called It's Just Lunch. The name captures a common line used by people who try to deny that there is any level of seriousness in getting together with a potential partner over a meal. If sharing food with another person did not suggest a relationship, we wouldn't feel the need to use a phrase such as "It's just lunch."

The truth is, even in our contemporary, fast-food society, sharing a meal with someone usually does suggest a relationship. When we want to deepen or solidify a relationship, we invite the other person to a meal. The more formal the food and the presentation of said food, the more formal the relationship. To be spotted at a Eucharistic meal should make people talk about us because it indicates that we are in a relationship that is scandalous in many ways. Through the act of celebrating the Eucharist, we are first and foremost proclaiming an intimacy with the creator of the universe. Talk about being a name-dropper! Perhaps even more scandalous, however, is that we are acknowledging deep ties to a coterie of questionable characters and, in fact, announcing that we are one of them: no better and possibly worse.

The Poultry Store

I grew up during the volatile and transitional decade of the 1960s, when this country shook loose the trappings of simpler times and embraced a rapidly changing culture. During this time of transition, I saw many anachronisms. Even in the inner city of Chicago where I grew up, I saw a horse-drawn carriage driven by a man selling produce. In the same decade, I witnessed the first man walking on the moon! Then there was the poultry store a few blocks from my home. Yes, in the heart of the hustle and bustle of the city, surrounded by contemporary department stores and businesses, our neighborhood still had a live-poultry store.

I remember walking past the windows of this store on my way to the grocery store and seeing live poultry in cages inside. And while I have no memory of my mother purchasing and preparing live poultry, it turns out that my wife, Joanne, who grew up in the same neighborhood, recalls going to that very same poultry store with her mother and grandmother, where they purchased a chicken or a duck, took it home, summarily executed it, drained it of blood, plucked off the feathers, and prepared it to eat. They represented the last vestiges of a time when people fully recognized that for humans to eat, something had to die. Not only did they recognize it, they participated in the "sacrifice" of the very animal they would later feast upon. (Make no mistake, even vegetarians require something to "die" in order to enjoy a meal.) Today, the sanitized manner in which food arrives on a plate in front of us, fully prepared, has removed any awareness of the connection between sacrifice and feasting. We no longer eat with the shadow of death lingering in the room.

And yet, this understanding of something needing to die in order that we may eat and live is at the very

"She just put two and two together, and figured out the sacrifice the turkey had to make in order for us to enjoy our Thanksgiving dinner."

heart of our understanding of the Eucharist. Not only is the Eucharist a meal and a memorial but it is also a sacrifice: for us to be fed, something—someone—had to die. For us to admit that we have been seeking to satisfy our cravings in the wrong way is painful. However, for us to unite with God, we must face up to this pain. For true "communion" to take place, there must be sacrifice.

The Sacrificial Lamb

For the people of Israel, this sacrifice was represented ritually through the offering of an animal in the Temple. Through this ritual sacrifice—the offering of the blood of a slaughtered animal—the Jewish people expressed the pain of facing up to their sinfulness and their desire to be in communion with God. On the Day of Atonement, the high priest would sprinkle this blood in the Holy of Holies and then sprinkle the blood on the people. As with the ancient (and unsanitary!) ritual of becoming "blood brothers" or "blood sisters" by pricking fingers and sharing blood, the people of Israel became "bonded" to God through the sharing of blood—fortunately, the blood of a slaughtered animal, not a slaughtered human being.

The first Christians, who were Jews, saw Jesus through this lens; he was the sacrificial lamb whose blood reunited them with God. John the Baptist, who was the son of a Temple priest, introduced Jesus to his disciples as the "Lamb of God," not to suggest that Jesus was cute and cuddly or meek and gentle but to point out that it will be through his blood that they (and we) will be saved. To this day, we are invited to Holy Communion through the words of John the Baptist, now spoken by our priests: "Behold the Lamb of God, behold him who takes away the sins of the world. Blessed are those called to the supper of the Lamb."

The Jewish people used to go to the Temple to have their sins forgiven, to be taught, and to be healed. In the Temple, Jesus boldly forgave sins, taught the word of God, and healed. He also boldly "cleansed the temple," driving out the money changers. He did this not simply because he was upset with shady business practices taking place in a house of prayer but rather to signify that this form of animal sacrifice was no longer needed since he was the Lamb of God to be sacrificed on behalf of the people. He announced that he would "destroy" the temple and rebuild it in three days, now claiming that his body is the new Temple, the locus of true sacrifice, and the place where true forgiveness, teaching, and healing will be accessed. At the Last Supper, Jesus used sacrificial language when he said that the bread is "my body, given up for you" and the cup of wine is "my blood, poured out for you"—referring to the great sacrifice of the Cross that would reconcile humankind to God.

The Mass—the celebration of the Eucharist—is our participation in this great sacrifice that unites us with God. This unity occurs not by a sprinkling of blood but through our consumption of the Body and Blood of Jesus. This also explains why the Catholic Mass is presided over by a priest and not just a preacher; what is being presided over is a sacrifice. It also explains why the priest members of my Doctor of Ministry class—friends such as Fr. John Breslin, Fr. Don Nevins, and Fr. David Hankus—do not wear their doctoral robes when presiding at Mass. Their primary role at Mass is not to be a professor giving a lecture but a priest presiding over a sacrifice. (More on this notion of the priest as presider over a sacrifice in chapter 8, "Living the Sacrament of Holy Orders.")

So Many Choices

I once had dinner at one of those Brazilian restaurants where servers walk around with platters of various meats inviting diners to choose which ones they want to sample. As they approach you, they identify what they're offering: maminha (sirloin steak), miolo da paleta (beef center cut), picanha (top sirloin), bife com alho (cut of beef), frango com bacon (chicken wrapped in bacon), sobre coxa (marinated chicken), and so on. Then they await your response: yes or no, depending on what you think will most satisfy your hunger.

When we come forward at Mass to receive Holy Communion, a similar dynamic takes place. The priest, deacon, or Extraordinary Minister of Holy Communion identifies what is being offered to us: "the Body of Christ" and "the Blood of Christ." Our response—"Amen"—is our declaration that this is indeed the only food and drink that will satisfy our hunger and thirst. To say *Amen* to the Body of Christ is to acknowledge that of all the options that life offers us, the Bread of Life is the only food that will satisfy our hungry hearts. To receive it is an expression of our unity with God and one another. To say *Amen* to the Cup that holds the Precious Blood of Jesus is to acknowledge that of all the options that this world offers us, the Blood of Christ—the very life of Jesus—is the only drink that will quench our spiritual thirst. To drink from the cup is an expression of our commitment to Christ's mission.

Thin Moments: Wine

Ordinary wine is part of many meals and many moments of relaxing and socializing. We have many opportunities to reflect on drinking from the Cup of Life:

> when we open and pour a bottle of wine
> when we are served a glass of wine
> when we take the first sip from a glass of wine
> when we get together with friends to share "spirits" with temperance
> when we eat grapes
> when we visit a winery or go on a wine-tasting tour
> when we set a dinner table and put out wine glasses
> when we are called on to make a toast

It Begins and Ends with Wine

It's interesting to note that in the Gospel of John, Jesus' public ministry begins and ends with wine. Near the beginning of John's Gospel (ch. 2), we find Jesus performing his first miracle: changing water into wine at the wedding feast at Cana. Near the end of John's Gospel (ch. 19), we find Jesus uttering the words "I am thirsty" as he is dying on the Cross. Immediately, someone soaks a sponge with common wine and lifts it to Jesus who, upon receiving it, says, "It is finished." Is this a coincidence? Not likely.

Celebrations are marked by abundance, and so when the wine supply ran low at the Wedding in Cana, the success of the wedding was in jeopardy. Jesus knew that he could use this moment to communicate something important about God: God provides and provides in abundance. It's miracle enough that Jesus changed water into wine, but even more significant is the amount of wine he created: six stone jars full, each capable of holding twenty to thirty gallons. That's a lot of wine! Not only did such an abundance of wine make for a good party, but it also told the guests—and us—that when Jesus is present, abundance is guaranteed. Notice that when Jesus fed the crowd of five thousand with five loaves of bread and two fish, the Apostles ended up with twelve baskets of leftovers. Jesus does not skimp! The Eucharist—and God's grace—are renewable sources of nourishment given to us in great abundance. The fact that Jesus sipped wine from a sponge while dying on the cross and then uttered the words "It is finished," symbolizes that the kingdom of God and its abundance of grace has become a reality.

But, EVERY Sunday?

We discussed in chapter 1 that we are a people "in recovery"—in need of a new narrative to replace the narrative of "stinking thinking" that led to our addiction to sin. In 12-step groups, one of the most critical components of this recovery is attending regular meetings. While a variety of reasons are given for the necessity of attending regular meetings, these are some of the most compelling:

➕ Addiction is a lonely, self-centered disease. It is important to find healing within the context of relationships that the meetings provide.

➕ It is important to share your recovery with newcomers lest they be left to fend for themselves.

The Mass

Catholics celebrate the Eucharist at Mass, the source and summit of our lives. As a ritual celebration, the Mass follows a pattern consisting of the following parts:

> Introductory Rites: opening procession, Penitential Rite, *Gloria*, opening prayer
> The Liturgy of the Word: first reading, responsorial psalm, second reading, Gospel, homily, Profession of Faith, general intercessions
> The Liturgy of the Eucharist: preparation of the gifts, prayer over the gifts, Eucharistic Prayer (Holy, Holy, Holy; Memorial Acclamation; Doxology), Communion Rite (the Lord's Prayer, the Sign of Peace, the Breaking of Bread, the Lamb of God or *Agnus Dei*, the reception of Holy Communion, prayer after Communion)
> Concluding Rites: blessing and dismissal

- ✚ Regular attendance at meetings keeps one focused on recovery, helps reduce relapse, and keeps one in his or her "right mind."
- ✚ Through regular attendance, one can find inspiration in the recovery of others.
- ✚ Meetings provide a safe and healthy environment for working on recovery.
- ✚ There is collective strength in people working together toward recovery in a group.
- ✚ We need the support of others when cravings arise.
- ✚ Regular attendance enables one to take stock of where he or she is in the recovery process.
- ✚ Isolation, which is at the heart of addictions, is overcome by regular attendance at meetings.
- ✚ Regular attendance enables one to go back to his or her humanity and focus on core values such as acceptance, faith, trust, honesty, courage, willingness, humility, forgiveness, freedom, perseverance, patience, and love.
- ✚ Addiction is chronic; one is never "cured."

I contend that each of the above compelling reasons for regularly attending and participating in 12-step meetings can and should be applied to attending and participating in a weekly celebration of the Eucharist. We go to Mass to be healed, to be saved, to experience "recovery" from our human addiction to sin.

Where Does the Word *Mass* Come From?

In the Latin Mass, the priest or deacon dismisses the assembly with the words "Ite, Missa Est!" which means, literally, "Go, (the assembly) is dismissed!" The word *Mass* comes from this Latin word *missa*, which means "sent" or "dismissed." The Mass, then, is the ritual celebration that sends us forth to proclaim to the world that the one and only thing that will satisfy our deep hunger is the Bread of Life, Jesus Christ!

I semi-facetiously tell parents that when their kids ask, "Why do we have to go to Mass?" they should respond by saying, "Because Mommy and Daddy are broken, and so are you. We go to Mass to get fixed. Get in the car." In essence, this is why we go. Of course, it helps if the music is joyful, the people are welcoming and participative, and the homily is good. But, in the end, we go to Mass for the same reason an addict goes to meetings: not for entertainment or for a feel-good experience but for recovery.

What Is the Real Presence of Jesus?

To the Hebrew mind, a living being was not thought of as a person within a body; the body and the person were one and the same. When Jesus offers us his body, he is offering us his being, his very personhood. Likewise, in Jewish thought, blood was believed to be the source of life. This is why the consumption of meat containing blood was prohibited—life is strictly God's domain. When Jesus offers us his blood, he invites us to "consume" his very life, to enter his domain. In essence, to receive the Eucharist is to be consumed with Jesus. Our being and life come into communion with Jesus' being and life. The real presence of Jesus means that we believe we are receiving Jesus' actual being and life, not just fondly recalling them. We refer to the transformation of bread and wine into the Body and Blood of Jesus as transubstantiation.

Real presence does not stop with Jesus in the Eucharist, however. As people nourished by the Eucharist, we are called to be truly present to those we encounter in our homes, workplaces, and communities. In each encounter we have, we can ask ourselves, "Am I offering a real presence to this person?"

> "The present moment is the only time over which we have dominion. The most important person is always the person you are with."
> —Thich Nhat Hanh, *The Miracle of Mindfulness*

Scripture

Jesus said to them, "Very truly I tell you, it is not Moses who has given you the bread from heaven, but it is my Father who gives you the true bread from heaven. For the bread of God is the bread that comes down from heaven and gives life to the world." "Sir," they said, "always give us this bread." Then Jesus declared, "I am the bread of life. Whoever comes to me will never go hungry, and whoever believes in me will never be thirsty." (JOHN 6:32–35)

Prayer

Loving God, I crave so many things. Too often, I look in all the wrong places and at all the wrong things to have my cravings filled. Help me recognize that, at my deepest level, I hunger for you. I desire your truth, beauty, and goodness. Thank you for the gift of your Son, Jesus Christ, the Bread of Life. Thank you, Jesus, for the gift of yourself in the Eucharist. May you always be the food that satisfies my hungry heart. Help me see the Eucharist as the key to my recovery from selfishness and lead me to a life of selflessness. Strengthened by your presence in me, may I offer real presence to those I encounter—a presence of compassion and mercy. Amen.

Chapter 5
Living the Sacrament of Reconciliation: Rescue Me!

"The whole power of the sacrament of Penance consists in restoring us to God's grace and joining us with him in an intimate friendship." Indeed, the sacrament of Reconciliation with God brings about a true "spiritual resurrection," restoration of the dignity and blessings of the life of the children of God, of which the most precious is friendship with God. (*Catechism of the Catholic Church*, no. 1468)

Where Is God When We Blunder?

It's not difficult to be more keenly aware of God's presence at moments when we encounter great beauty or overwhelming joy. It may come as a surprise, then, to discover that our awareness of God's presence can increase in moments of failure, defeat, or loss, those times when it seems that God is nowhere to be found. It might take the perspective of another human being at such moments to help us recognize that we are not alone; God is near.

When God is nearby at moments of failure, he is not there to say "I told you so" or to punish us or, worse yet, to laugh at us the way Nelson, a character on *The Simpsons*, seems to be around to say "Ha-Ha!" every time someone commits a blunder. And let's face it, humankind has committed more than our fair share of dramatic blunders, many of which are recorded in the Bible. Time and again, Scripture reveals a loving God who extends invitation after invitation to his people to enter a faithful relationship, only

> **Our awareness of God's presence can increase in moments of failure, defeat, or loss, those times when it seems that God is nowhere to be found.**

to be rejected time after time. And while the Bible does reveal stories of the wrath of God (more about that later), the overall thrust of God's response to humankind's pattern of committing major blunders is one of mercy, forgiveness, and compassion—or rescue, restoration, and reassurance.

Sin—One Little Typo Can Change Everything

You may have noticed that talking about sin has gone out of style. One of the reasons for this is that, over time, we have blown the whole concept of sin out of proportion. At the mention of the word *sin*, most people conjure up notions of heinous deeds that warrant prison time in this life and an eternity of hell in the life to come. And, while some sinful acts such as murder and theft are indeed dramatic, the average person does not commit such atrocities. Thus, discussing the concept of sin is dismissed as fearmongering. In Scripture, however, sin is understood as "missing the mark." In fact, the Greek word for sin, *hamartia*, is a term from the world of archery; it literally means "missing the mark."

Now, thinking of sin as "missing the mark" is not to minimize the seriousness of sin. One small act that misses the mark can have serious ramifications, just as the following typo dramatically changes the meaning of the statement:

> Let's eat Grandpa.
> Let's eat, Grandpa.

One small typo—the absence of a comma—changes an invitation to your grandpa to dine together into an invitation to others to engage in an act of cannibalism with your grandpa as the main course. To miss the mark when it comes to following God's will does indeed have serious consequences. Few of us choose to do evil. However, we make choices all the time that, while on the surface appear to be just fine, in reality miss the mark. Sometimes, the consequences of missing the mark are immediately recognizable. Other times, the consequences are less obvious until they have a cumulative effect. Just as writers need editors and proofreaders to help them recognize the error of their ways, we need a perspective

> We need a perspective beyond our own to help us recognize how we have missed the mark when it comes to following God's will.

beyond our own to help us recognize how we have missed the mark when it comes to following God's will and to help us recognize just how serious the ramifications for missing the mark will be. We need an intervention.

We Need an Intervention

When a child gets himself or herself into a predicament—getting his or her head stuck between the railings on a staircase, for example—an adult has to intervene to rescue the child. When adults fall prey to an addiction that gets out of control, other adults may stage an intervention to put the person on a path to sobriety. In a similar way, we human beings who are prone to missing the mark need constant intervention. Thankfully, God has recognized this and has repeatedly intervened in the lives of his people, beginning with Israel and culminating in the sending of his only Son, Jesus, to be one of us. Our Baptism is not the guarantee of a life without the selfish blunders we call sin but is the acceptance of God's intervention through Jesus Christ—an intervention that provides us with a way out of the messes we create.

If Jesus' mission can be summed up in one word, it is *reconciliation*; he intervened in human history to rescue and restore us and now reassures us by promising to remain with us throughout our "recovery" until the end of time. For God, reconciliation is nothing less than rescue. All of us can recall watching footage on TV of heroic rescues as a victim finds himself or herself in swirling flood

> **The greatest rescue story is the rescue of all humankind by Jesus Christ.**

waters. The rescuer enters the swirling torrents and extricates the flailing victim, carrying him or her to safety. It is no coincidence, then, that the Bible tells us the story of Noah and the flood—God's first rescue story—to illustrate that he alone can save us from the torrents of sin. Indeed, the Bible is full of rescue stories, including Daniel's rescue from the lions' den, Jonah's rescue from the belly of the whale, and of course, God's rescue of the Jewish people from slavery in Egypt. The greatest rescue story, however, is the rescue of all humankind by Jesus Christ.

A Savior

Bishop Robert Barron often remarks on the importance of seeing Jesus, not just as a helpful teacher, a wise philosopher, or a swell guy but as a Savior, a rescuer. Barron illustrates this by inviting us to imagine ourselves sinking in a pit of quicksand: do we need a teacher, a philosopher, or a swell guy to come along? No, we need a savior! Someone to pull us out of the muck!

In a study published in *The Journal of Positive Psychology*, researchers studied what caused some people to rescue Jews during the Holocaust while others turned a blind eye. It turned out that those who rescued others at great personal risk and with no expectation of reward did so not because of factors such as wealth, prominence, convenience, or proximity but solely because their character reflected high levels of social responsibility, empathy, risk-taking, and compassion in the face of human suffering. These are all divine qualities, characteristics of a God who always seeks to be in relationship with his people, feels our pain, and risks becoming one of us in order to rescue us and restore us to intimacy with him. That is the heart of reconciliation.

> "With Jesus, God's rescue operation has been put into effect once and for all."
> —N. T. WRIGHT, *SIMPLY CHRISTIAN: WHY CHRISTIANITY MAKES SENSE*

Reconciliation: The Mission of God

In a 2005 paper, *Reconciliation as the Mission of God*, forty-seven Christian leaders across the world wrote, "The mission of God in our fallen, broken world is reconciliation." Of course, St. Paul made it abundantly clear that Jesus' mission was centered on the notion of reconciliation.

> Therefore, if anyone is in Christ, he is a new creation; the old has gone, the new has come! All this is from God, who *reconciled* us to himself through Christ and gave us the ministry of *reconciliation*: that God was *reconciling* the world to himself in Christ, not counting men's sins against them. And he has committed to us the message of *reconciliation*. We are therefore Christ's ambassadors, as though God were making his appeal through us. We implore you on Christ's behalf: Be *reconciled* to God. God made him who had no sin to be sin for us, so that in him we might become the righteousness of God. (2 Corinthians 5:16–21, NIV)

The concept of reconciliation remains elusive in our world, which often seems more interested in conquest. A quick glance at the headlines in today's online news stories reflects this through the following attention-grabbing words to describe one person publicly criticizing another: *eviscerates, destroys, demolishes, obliterates, disembowels, smashes, slams, decimates, annihilates, torches, castrates, thrashes, slams, mauls, hammers, rips,* and several others I can't print here. Jesus, on the other hand, introduces a vocabulary of reconciliation that includes words such as mercy, forgiveness, compassion, meekness, pity, peace, comfort, and, of course, love.

To reconcile means to restore, to put back together that which has become separated or fractured. To reconcile is to restore harmony and balance. In economic terms, to reconcile is to make sure that one's columns are balanced. If the columns are out of balance, this suggests an amount is due and that amount must be covered. I'm sure you've had the experience of covering someone's shortfall or someone covering your shortfall when settling the check at a restaurant. In our shortfall with God—when we come up short in our response to God's loving invitation—Jesus covers our shortfall and reconciles us with the Father.

> **The Sacrament of Reconciliation is one of the ways that God's intervention continues to play out in our lives.**

God's intervention to rescue us was indeed set into motion with the birth of Jesus, the Incarnation, when heaven and earth intersected once and for all and were reconciled. Jesus, in turn, remains with us throughout our recovery through the Holy Spirit, through Baptism, through the Eucharist, and through the Sacrament of Reconciliation. While Baptism is our acceptance of God's intervention and the Eucharist is the ongoing support we need during our recovery, the Sacrament of Reconciliation is there for us when we "fall off the wagon" and go back to our habits that miss the mark. The Sacrament of Reconciliation is one of the ways that God's intervention continues to play out in our lives. We have a continuous need to overcome the human tendency to live contrary to the divine will, a will that compels us to live a life of selfless love.

The Sacrament of Reconciliation

- Reconciliation
- Penance
- Penance and Reconciliation
- Confession

These four terms all refer to the same experience of being rescued, restored, and reassured by Jesus through confession to a priest. The *Catechism of the Catholic Church* refers to this sacrament as the Sacrament of Penance and Reconciliation (no. 1440). For the sake of convenience, we shall refer to it as the Sacrament of Reconciliation.

The Gospels reveal, time and time again, Jesus showing mercy (forgiving sins). Even as he was dying on the cross, Jesus uttered words of forgiveness: "Father, forgive them, for they know not what they do" (Luke 23:34). It is Jesus' forgiveness that we embrace in Baptism when we die to sin and rise again to new life in Jesus. Baptism, however, is not the end of our conversion experience but the beginning of ongoing conversion in Jesus Christ. And so, when we sin, which we unfortunately continue to do even after Baptism, we are invited to renew our Baptism through the Sacrament of Reconciliation and to experience anew God's mercy.

Let's Get Real

"Why do I need to go to a priest to have my sins forgiven?" This is the question that gets to the heart of the Catholic understanding of forgiveness. It also is a question that many Protestants ask of Catholics. The answer is quite simple. First, we Catholics do indeed believe that Jesus forgave sin once and for all from the Cross and that, in Baptism, we have found salvation and forgiveness of sins. When we sin, we can and should go to our room and ask the Lord for forgiveness. At this point, however, Catholics take it further. Remember, we are a sacramental church, meaning that we express outwardly and tangibly what is happening in the intangible world of our spiritual lives. The act of going to a priest, verbally naming the sin—making it tangible—and hearing the words of forgiveness spoken by the priest ("I absolve you in the name of the Father, and of the Son, and of the Holy Spirit") are outward signs of the inner world of sin and forgiveness.

> The Sacrament of Penance and Reconciliation, like all sacraments, is efficacious: it achieves that which it expresses.

Think of it this way. If someone you are in love with never says "I love you," then that love suffers. The words "I love you" are efficacious: they achieve the effect they express. The same is true for the words "I'm sorry" and "I forgive you." If someone you are in love with cannot say the words "I'm sorry" or "I forgive you," then the relationship suffers. Saying the words "I'm sorry" or "I forgive you" completes the experience of reconciling a relationship. All of this applies to our Catholic understanding of forgiveness in the Sacrament of Reconciliation. Unless we can name our sins and say the words "I'm sorry" and hear the words of Jesus spoken—"I forgive you"— our relationship with Jesus and others suffers. The Sacrament of Reconciliation, like all sacraments, is efficacious: it achieves that which it expresses.

The Seal of Confession

In the Sacrament of Penance and Reconciliation, the dignity of the person is of the greatest importance. The priest is bound to absolute secrecy regarding the sins confessed to him. This secrecy is called the "sacramental seal." (*Catechism of the Catholic Church*, no. 1467)

Naming the Sin

The wisdom of naming the sin can also be found in the 12-step approach to overcoming addictions. The founders of the 12 steps recognized that unless the sin or addiction is named and revealed to at least one other person, the healing cannot truly begin—the moment cannot truly become "thin" because of the thickness of that which remains unspoken or unnamed. Without naming the sin or the addiction and sharing it with someone, the individual runs the risk of living in denial, which prevents true healing from beginning.

All of this leads to an interesting point. Over the past few decades, the number of people going to confession has dramatically decreased. This is because some see this sacrament as unnecessary or antiquated. During that same period, however, the number of people naming their sins in 12-step programs or entering therapy dramatically increased. The bottom line is this: people need healing. We need to reclaim the profound wisdom inherent in the Sacrament of Reconciliation and help people recognize the great benefits of talking about our sinfulness with another human being— the priest—and hearing the words of forgiveness spoken out loud in a human voice.

The Liturgy of Reconciliation

Ordinarily, the Sacrament of Reconciliation includes the following elements:

> greeting and blessing from the priest
> confession of sins by the penitent
> the giving and accepting of a penance
> an act of contrition
> the priest's absolution
> a proclamation of praise by the penitent
> dismissal of the penitent by the priest

It's Not about You

Remember how we said that a small typo can make a big difference? That is obvious when we recognize how easy it would be to misspell the word *selfless* and instead type the word *selfish*. In fact, the difference between the words *selfless* and *selfish* is as vast as night and day and can result in our either hitting the target or missing the mark.

If there is one thing that Christianity reminds us about over and over, it is the notion that "it's not about you." The truth is, we are born into this world thinking that it is all about us. Human beings are naturally self-centered. As babies, we cry and scream to be held, fed, and rocked to sleep. We learn the words "me" and "mine" before the words "you" and "yours," and we understand the concept of "keep" before we learn the concept of "share."

As we grow older, our parents teach us gradually to accept the fact that the universe does not revolve around us.

Jesus came to teach us that the key to eternal life is to "die" to our self-centeredness—our old self—and to be born again as someone whose central focus is the good of others. The Cross is the ultimate symbol of selfless love. Shortly before his Death on that Cross, Jesus showed us that washing the feet of others was the hallmark of discipleship.

Unfortunately, we often miss the mark when it comes to Jesus' directive to live lives that are centered on God and others. As Bishop Robert Barron writes in *The Strangest Way*, "Either your life is about Jesus and his mission [to serve others] or it is about you. There is no third option." And it is that first option—a life that is about Jesus and his mission to serve others—that is the only surefire way to a fulfilled life. The second option misses the mark and results in a life that is broken and in need of repairs that can be effected only by God!

When coaches help athletes overcome a tendency to miss the mark, they help them recognize what they are doing wrong, show them how to correct it, and give them another chance to get it right. When it comes to sin—the ways we miss the mark when it comes to following God's will—God acts in a similar manner as a coach: he helps us recognize what we have done wrong, reveals to us the correct path, and then empowers us to forge ahead, trying once again to hit the mark with God's assistance. When we do indeed "hit the mark"—when our will aligns with God's will—we

Thin Moments: Reconciliation

The following everyday occurrences can serve as opportunities for you to reflect on the riches of the Sacrament of Reconciliation:

> when you see a rescue on TV or in the movies
> when you "miss the mark" while aiming for something such as playing darts
> when someone covers for you when you're short or when you do the same for another
> when you restore or polish wood or clean a window
> when you hear or say the words "I'm sorry"
> when you balance your checkbook or reconcile your sales ledger or other account
> when you set aside your own needs to care for the needs of another (or someone does the same for you)
> when someone goes out of his or her way to treat you like one of the family
> when you take a shower or bath or wash clothes that were especially dirty
> when you restore life to a plant, flower, or lawn that has gone dry

are in the state of grace. When we miss the mark—when we follow our own will instead of the will of God—we venture into the reality known as sin.

Grace and Sin

Although we don't want to wallow in our sinfulness, without some understanding of sin we have no need to be rescued! What we need is a healthy understanding of sin, a healthy dose of fear, a healthy dose of guilt, and above all, a healthy understanding of grace and mercy, both of which trump the preceding.

So, if sin is about missing the mark, grace is about hitting the target. Grace is not a quantifiable reality. It is not something that we store up. Grace is a relationship—namely, a relationship with God. When we are in the state of grace, we are in a healthy relationship with God, filled with God's life. For example, when we say "Hail Mary, full of grace," we are saying that Mary is filled with God's life and that she is in a deeply intimate relationship with God.

> "Grace is not a strange, magic substance which is subtly filtered into our souls to act as a kind of spiritual penicillin. Grace is unity, oneness within ourselves, oneness with God."
> —Thomas Merton

Grace is not something that we earn. It is a gift from God. God graces us with his presence. We can accept that relationship, we can ignore it, or, worse yet, we can reject it. In Baptism, we have been gifted with God's grace. We have been welcomed into an intimate relationship with the Divine.

Sin: When We Tell God to Wait in the Car

Now, with grace as our backdrop, we can return to the concept of sin or missing the mark. Sin is the ignoring, injuring, or rejecting of our relationship with God. Because those words sound so dramatic, I like to use the image of sin as those times when we tell God to "wait in the car" while we do or say something we'd prefer he not see. Sin does not stop with our relationship with God, however. God has indicated clearly that loving him is inseparable from loving our neighbor; sin is also the ignoring, injuring, or rejecting of our relationship with others.

Sins of Omission

While we tend to focus on our actions as the ways we miss the mark, sometimes we miss the mark through inaction. Jesus provided us with a great example of what we call "sins of omission" in the parable of the rich man and Lazarus (not the Lazarus he raised from the dead) in Luke 16:19-31. The rich man in the story doesn't do anything directly to harm poor Lazarus, who sits at his gate. Rather, it is the fact that the rich man ignores the plight of Lazarus that makes him guilty of sin. We pray for forgiveness from sins of commission and omission at Mass when, in the Penitential Rite, we ask forgiveness "for what I have done and for what I have failed to do." By failing to act, we miss the mark.

Missing the mark can sometimes be minor; at other times it can be dangerous, such as when an archer misses the target altogether and injures a bystander! When we ignore or injure our relationship with God or others, we call these sins venial, which means that they are less serious but still harmful. Venial sins are not to be confused with mistakes or accidents, however.

+ A mistake is an unintentional error in judgment, such as mistaking salt for sugar and mixing it in your coffee.

+ An accident is something that happens unintentionally or unexpectedly, such as talking with our hands and hitting someone in the face because we didn't know they were walking by at that moment.

Some mistakes and accidents have serious or even tragic consequences. But a sin, whether less or more serious, involves will and intent.

Venial sins are intentional actions that are misguided, resulting in injury to a relationship. When we reject our relationship with God and others, we call this a mortal sin because it "kills" or cuts off our relationship with God from our end. For a sin to be mortal, three conditions must apply:

+ it must be a very serious offense (serious matter)

+ the person must know how serious the sin is (full knowledge)

+ the person must freely choose to do it anyway (full consent)

The Necessary Ingredients

The Sacrament of Reconciliation includes the following:

> **Contrition:** We identify our sins (through an examination of conscience), express sincere sorrow for our sins, and commit ourselves not to repeat them.
> **Confession:** We name the sins aloud to the priest.
> **Absolution:** We are set free (loosened) from our sins by the priest through the words of absolution.
> **Satisfaction:** We strive to repair the damage our sins have caused by performing works of penance.

Being Treated Like One of the Family

Our discussion of sin and grace would be incomplete if we did not spend a few moments talking about mercy. The first word of our discussion about sin was *grace*, and the last word of this discussion is *mercy*. We begin and end with God. Sin is what gets in the way of grace and mercy. Unfortunately, when we think of the word *mercy*, we often think of someone groveling before an evil villain, crying out for his or her life to be spared. We do not have to beg for God's mercy; God offers it as a gift. *Mercy* is another word for compassion or kindness that is directed toward an offender. Mercy is what God always offers to us, despite our offenses. Sin is not the end of the story. Mercy is what awaits us. God's merciful love calls us out of sin and redeems us—saves us, delivers us—from every evil and restores us to grace. When we respond to God's mercy with repentance and contrition, we are restored to grace: our relationship with God is deepened. When we pray for God's mercy, we are praying for the grace we need to accept what God is always offering.

A good way to understand mercy is to reflect on this image of a classic 19th-century American painting by Frederick Cotman titled *One of the Family*, which depicts a farming family gathered around their dining-room table enjoying a sumptuous meal. At the center of the painting is the mother of the family, who is craning her neck to turn around and offer a handful of food from the table to the family horse, who has stuck his neck through the top part of the door. The mother is treating the horse like one of the family. In Hebrew, the word for mercy—*rechem*—is also the word for womb, which means that to treat someone with mercy is to treat them as if they were a child of your womb. This is how God treats us. To be reconciled with God is to once again be part of the family and to feel the intimacy of God's parental love.

True Peace Requires Restorative Justice

Just as good physical health is more than the absence of sickness and injury, true spiritual health is more than the avoidance of sinful acts; it also entails acts of virtue that hit the mark. Because our sinful acts cause disruption in relationships, reconciliation actively seeks to restore such relationships. Establishing and maintaining peace requires hard work that is focused on healing and making amends. Reconciliation is not just a private act of self-improvement but a communal effort to be a reconciling people working toward a just world. Too often, our understanding of justice is one that is punitive. Scriptural justice—the justice of God—is primarily restorative: the focus is not so much on the punishment of the perpetrator but on the restoration of the victim and the perpetrator to right relationship.

> "Reconciliation is the center and perennial test of faith."
> —JOHN DE GRUCHY,
> *RECONCILIATION: RESTORING JUSTICE*

It is for this reason that the priest assigns a penance in the Sacrament of Reconciliation: a symbolic action on our part to restore that which has been broken. Therefore, it makes great sense for parishes to celebrate the Sacrament of Reconciliation for groups of people who are about to engage in service projects and works of mercy; the sacrament can help us see our works of mercy as part of God's plan for restorative justice and admit that we ourselves have contributed, either directly or indirectly, to the injustice we are seeking to remedy.

As soon as she finished college, Laura left her small hometown and went to the big city, where she became a successful performer in show business. Eventually, she returned to her hometown for a visit and on a Saturday afternoon went to confession at the church she attended as a child. In the confessional, her old pastor, Fr. Sullivan, recognized her voice and asked with great excitement and curiosity about her work as a performer. When Laura explained that she was an acrobatic dancer, Fr. Sullivan asked her if she would be kind enough to demonstrate her talent. Happy to oblige, Laura stepped out of the confessional and went into a series of cartwheels, leaping splits, handsprings, and backflips. Across the church, two older women were awaiting their turn to go to confession to Fr. Turner. Upon witnessing Laura's acrobatics, one said to the other, "Precisely why I never go to confession to Fr. Sullivan. Look at the penance he's handing out these days!"

Repentance

In the movie *As Good as It Gets*, Melvin, a cranky, obsessive-compulsive author (played by Jack Nicholson), says to the waitress he is attracted to (played by Helen Hunt): "You make me want to be a better man." Often, when we encounter someone with qualities we admire, we become more aware of our own shortcomings—and our desire for improvement. Becoming a disciple of Jesus works the same way. When we accept Jesus' invitation to discipleship, we encounter his great mercy, which, in turn, makes us more aware of our shortcomings and our desire to be a better person. We cannot help but ask for forgiveness and for the grace we need to move forward. Walking with Jesus makes us want to be better people.

The only authentic response to encountering Jesus, therefore, is true conversion. Unfortunately, because of our limited understanding of the word *conversion*, we often feel that we haven't experienced, are not experiencing, and will not be experiencing conversion anytime soon. But in truth, conversion is always at hand. It is our ever-present access to God's new story line for our lives. All we need to do is to redefine *conversion* as that

> **The only authentic response to encountering Jesus, therefore, is true conversion.**

which happens to us during the thin moments of life when we come face-to-face with the realization that we are incapable of sustaining ourselves and need to turn to God, who alone can rescue, restore, and reassure us.

At the intersection of heaven and earth, we find peace. It doesn't take much for us, however, to miss the mark, to lose our sense of direction, and to find our way onto detours and dead ends. Through the Sacrament of Reconciliation, we can once again "check in" at the intersection of heaven and earth where God awaits to restore us.

Scripture

"Come now, let us settle the matter,"
says the LORD.
"Though your sins are like scarlet,
they shall be as white as snow;
though they are red as crimson,
they shall be like wool."
(ISAIAH 1:18)

Prayer

Merciful Father, rescue me from myself. Rescue me from my misplaced desires and from my tendency to think that it's all about me. I'm in need of an intervention–a divine intervention–lest I continue missing the mark. Help me find my way back to the intersection of heaven and earth: the place you introduced me to in Baptism. Give me the courage to name my sins and to accept your mercy and forgiveness. Then, healed by your grace, send me forth as your ambassador, bringing your reconciliation to those who need it most. Amen.

Chapter 6
Living the Sacrament of the Anointing of the Sick: Healing as God's M.O.

Illness and suffering have always been among the gravest problems confronted in human life. In illness, man experiences his powerlessness, his limitations, and his finitude. Every illness can make us glimpse death. Illness can lead to anguish, self-absorption, sometimes even despair and revolt against God. It can also make a person more mature, helping him discern in his life what is not essential so that he can turn toward that which is. Very often illness provokes a search for God and a return to him. (*Catechism of the Catholic Church*, no. 1500-1501)

What Is Health?

Are you healthy? That's a tough question to answer because health can be rather nebulous. It's much easier to identify sickness. We know when we have a fever, aches and pains, an upset stomach, or a dry, hacking cough. Is health simply the absence of sickness? Too often, we define things by what they are not, such as defining peace as the absence of war. In the same way, health is much more than the absence of illness, injury, or pain.

Some years ago, I was experiencing a lack of health. I woke up each morning feeling tired and sick. I had generalized aches and pains and episodes of light-headedness. I began missing days of work and visited several doctors to undergo a variety of tests in search of what could possibly be causing me to feel so sick for so long. As each test came back negative, my wife, Joanne, would rejoice, telling me that I was healthy. I, on the other hand, would be disappointed because I still felt sick even though, "on paper," I was completely healthy. After eliminating every possible physical cause for my unhealthy state of being, it dawned on me that perhaps I was

Living the Sacrament of the Anointing of the Sick: Healing as God's M.O.

[81]

limiting myself to only one dimension of human health: the physical. After consulting with some close friends, including my good friend Fr. Frank, it became obvious that the cause of my illness was only partly physical and was primarily emotional and spiritual: I was depressed. While my return to health involved medicine for the chemical imbalance of depression, it also involved counseling and spiritual direction so that I could achieve the harmony and balance that is good health.

So, once again, health is much more than the absence of illness, injury, or pain. It is a harmony—a balance—of our physical, emotional, psychological, and spiritual dimensions. It is wholeness. Interestingly, the etymology of the word *health* reveals that it means not only wholeness but also holiness, and, of course, to be holy is to be like God, who alone is perfect harmony and balance.

> **Health is much more than the absence of illness, injury, or pain. It is a harmony—a balance—of our physical, emotional, psychological, and spiritual dimensions.**

Finding God When Things Fall Apart

When we talk about "thin places" or "thin moments"—when the veil between heaven and earth seems very thin—we tend to think of places of great beauty or experiences of joy or accomplishment. But thin moments are not limited to experiences of beauty and joy. The truth is, we come face-to-face with mystery at moments of loss or pain. This is why people have long identified late autumn, when we experience the loss of warmth and sunlight, as a thin moment that brings us closer to those who have crossed over from this life to the next. The celebrations of Halloween, All Saints Day, and All Souls Day/Dia de los Muertos are at the time of the year when we are enveloped in ever-increasing darkness and the "death" of nature. In a similar way, we can and should encounter mystery in our lives during moments of loss. Sickness, the loss of our health, is one of those moments: it is an

"Grandpa, Mommy says Anointing of the Sick is when you get Jesus as your doctor. . . and He doesn't give you any shots or icky medicine!"

experience that makes us deeply aware of our mortality, our reason for living, and the question of whether God is present when things fall apart and we are powerless to remedy the situation on our own.

Sickness and Powerlessness

Nobody likes feeling powerless, such as when a child is bullied, when an adult faces job loss and mounting bills, or when an elderly person must give up his or her driver's license because of diminishing abilities. Perhaps the worst feeling of powerlessness is when you find yourself lying in a hospital bed, unsure of your prognosis. In my book *Under the Influence of Jesus,* I refer to **sickness** (of body and mind) as one of the "big four" realities— along with **lack of sustenance** (job, food, housing), **natural disasters**, and **death**—that precipitate a feeling of powerlessness. These big four are all-too-familiar reminders of the presence of evil and all that is in opposition to God. At the same time, they are experiences that raise questions about the presence and power of God in response to such evil. Despite the advances of science and technology, we recognize that the power to overcome these realities and the threats they pose often lies beyond our capacity. This explains why people often turn to God when confronted by one or more of the big four.

It is no coincidence, then, that Jesus' miracles focused on these four realities.

➕ He healed the sick and drove out demons (sickness of body and mind).

➕ He changed water to wine and multiplied loaves and fishes (lack of sustenance).

➕ He calmed storms and walked on water (natural disasters).

➕ He raised the dead (death).

The message of Jesus' miracles is clear: Jesus embodies the power of God, the healer. Jesus' name—*Yeshua*, in Hebrew—literally means "God saves," which, as we have indicated, is synonymous with "God heals." We will

> **Sickness is an experience that makes us deeply aware of our mortality, our reason for living, and the question of whether God is present when things fall apart and we are powerless to remedy the situation on our own.**

Living the Sacrament of the Anointing of the Sick: Healing as God's M.O.

[83]

limit our focus in this book to the first of those big four—sickness—and see how Jesus' healing is the foundation for the Sacrament of the Anointing of the Sick.

Sickness Is Contrary to God's Desires

Before we go any further, let's get one thing straight: while it's true that being sick is no fun, we have to stop telling people that their sickness is their "cross to bear" as if God assigns illnesses to people. When Jesus said that anyone who wishes to be his disciple must pick up his cross and follow him, he was not suggesting that illness was one way of doing that. While it is true that we can find meaning in our suffering by uniting it with Jesus' suffering on the Cross, this is not the cross that Jesus was referring to when he spoke of the requirements for discipleship. The cross that disciples must bear is the pain that one endures precisely for claiming to be a follower of Jesus. Sickness, on the other hand, is a burden that Jesus wishes to relieve. Living with illness is contrary to both our desires and God's.

> Sickness is a burden that Jesus wishes to relieve.

In the Gospels, Jesus cures the following types of physical maladies: fever, paralysis, blindness, leprosy, dropsy, hemorrhaging, deafness, and muteness. Each of these healings is a sign that God is on our side in our fight against these intrusions into his creation. Jesus did not wipe out all disease and illness; that remains for the end of time. However, he did make it clear that we are not alone, nor are we powerless, when we face these maladies. God, our healer, is with us. These healings also speak to us on a symbolic level; we may be experiencing spiritual forms of paralysis, blindness, deafness, and so on. If Jesus can cure these maladies on the physical level, he is certainly capable of curing them on other levels that are less visible.

> "Jesus did not promise to take away our burdens. He promised to help us carry them."
> —Joseph Cardinal Bernardin

Like Father, Like Son

In biblical times, it was common for the firstborn son to take up his father's trade. Jesus was no exception: like his earthly father, Joseph, he took up carpentry. Like his heavenly Father, however, he became a healer. We think of Jesus primarily as a teacher and rightly so since he was often referred to as teacher or rabbi by his disciples. His disciples could just as easily have referred to him as "doctor," as in "physician." Jesus implied that this title would be appropriate for himself when he said, "It is not the healthy who need a doctor but the sick. I have not come to call the righteous but sinners" (Mark 2:17). Jesus devoted a large percentage of his time and energy to those who were sick. It is safe to say that the apple did not fall far from the tree: Jesus, like his Father, is a healer, and he expects his followers to be the same. So where does this notion of God being primarily a healer come from? From God himself.

In the story of the Exodus event, after God had led his people out of slavery in Egypt to freedom through the parting of the Red Sea, the Hebrew people wanted to know more about this awesome God with a mysterious name of YHWH or "I Am Who Am." Like people in a superhero story asking, "Who was that masked man?" the people of Israel wanted to know precisely who it was that defeated Pharaoh and his armies, parted the Red Sea, and led them to freedom from slavery. At the first opportunity that presented itself, as the people of Israel began their desert journey, God revealed his identity to his people:

> "If you listen carefully to the Lord your God and do what is right in his eyes, if you pay attention to his commands and keep all his decrees, I will not bring on you any of the diseases I brought on the Egyptians, **for I am the Lord, who heals you**." (Exodus 15:26; NIV)

In some translations, the last line of that verse is, "for I am the Lord, your healer." Thus, one of the very first ways that God describes himself is "healer," aka "doctor" or "physician." God wants his people to know that, first and foremost, he is the one who brings health and prosperity—harmony and balance (not to be confused with financial prosperity)—to his people as long as they call on him for help and abide by his will. Healing is what God does. A healer is who God is. In fact, in Scripture, God often refers to Israel's suffering in medical terms:

Living the Sacrament of the Anointing of the Sick: Healing as God's M.O.

[85]

Is there no balm in Gilead?
> Is there no physician there?
Why then is there no healing
> for the wound of my people?
(Jeremiah 8:22)

The balm is a medicinal term referring to an ointment or salve that heals open wounds. The contemporary equivalent would be if God were to ask, in reference to violence in a major city, "Is there no Bacitracin in Chicago?" or "Is there no ibuprofen in Los Angeles?" "Aren't there any doctors there?" "Who is there to bring healing to my people?" Healing is what God wants most for his people.

> **Healing is what God does. A healer is who God is.**

Healing Is God's M.O.

Think of it this way. If you were hired by a company whose CEO asked that you devote three to four full days of each week (60–80 percent of your time) accompanying him or her to various hospitals to visit the sick, you would conclude that caring for the sick was a major priority of this company no matter what else it produced or provided. A close look at Scripture reveals that a large percentage of the Gospels pertain to Jesus healing others: it was not a sideline for Jesus nor was it tangential to his message: healing was integral to Jesus' mission of carrying out his Father's will. Healing was an essential dimension of his ministry.

> **Healing was an essential dimension of Jesus' ministry.**

Compassionate care, then, is Jesus' M.O., or modus operandi, his way of proceeding. In fact, the Gospels tell us that Jesus performed miracles of healing not out of an egotistical need to show off his power but rather because he was often moved with pity for those who were suffering. The Greek words for "moved with pity" suggest much more than a sentimental reaction but convey that he had been "kicked in the gut" by the spectacle of human beings suffering. It is no coincidence, then, that as Jesus sends out his disciples, he sends them out to "proclaim the kingdom of God and to heal." (Luke 9:2). Through his words and actions, Jesus reveals to us that healing is an essential expression of God's compassionate care for his people, something the Father revealed to his people centuries earlier when he said, "I am God, your healer." Sickness and the suffering that accompanies it is not just a "kick in the gut" for us humans but also for God whose compassion for us comes from his "gut," his deepest core.

Continuing Jesus' Mission of Healing

When someone is sick, why do we send flowers? Or fruit arrangements? Or chocolates? In what way can a bunch of daisies, some watermelon and cantaloupe, or a few chocolate-covered cherries bring about healing at the molecular level? For the answer to that, go back to the question we began with in chapter 1: does kissing an "ouchie" really make it better? We humans are very complex beings whose emotional, intellectual, spiritual, and physical realities are all woven together. Catholic anthropology rejects a dualism between body and spirit. As a result, we know that physical illness has emotional and spiritual implications. Physical illness brings us face-to-face with our mortality, our fragility, and our vulnerability. In other words, it makes us afraid, and fear is the opposite of faith. When we are filled with fear, we are unable to trust. And when we are unable to trust, we are unable to hope. And without hope, healing is impeded if not completely blocked.

> Since most of us do not have the medical skills to treat the physical reality of illness, we respond by seeking to address the related emotional, psychological, and spiritual realities.

Since most of us do not have the medical skills to treat the physical reality of illness, we respond by seeking to address the related emotional, psychological, and spiritual realities. For Catholics, our approach to healing goes beyond sending flowers, fruit arrangements, or chocolates, as wonderful as those all are, and incorporates sign, symbol, and ritual in the Sacrament of the Anointing of the Sick.

The Sacrament of the Anointing of the Sick, like all the sacraments, is an encounter with Christ our healer. It is an encounter with Jesus when we need him most: when we are on the threshold of faith or despair, trust or fear. The Sacrament of the Anointing of the Sick is a sacrament of healing (see James 5:13–15). There's no magic involved. Just as illness affects us at the physical, spiritual, and emotional levels, so does healing. Encountering Jesus and his narrative of compassion and mercy (of rescue, restoration, and

The Liturgy of the Anointing of the Sick

Years ago, the Anointing of the Sick was considered a private matter between the priest and the sick person. Today, however, the Church emphasizes the communal nature of the sacrament and encourages family and friends to be present for the ritual, which includes the following:

> a Penitential Rite

> Liturgy of the Word

> laying on of hands: the priest lays his hands on the head of the sick person

> anointing with the oil of the sick: the priest anoints the forehead and hands of the sick person and says, "Through this holy anointing may the Lord in his love and mercy help you with the grace of the Holy Spirit. May the Lord who frees you from sin save you and raise you up." (*Catechism of the Catholic Church*, no. 513)

> viaticum: for those who are near death, the priest offers the Sacrament of Penance and Reconciliation and the Eucharist (*viaticum* means food for the journey)

reassurance) lifts our hearts and fills us with confidence, trust, and hope. This spiritual healing can and often does bring about healing on the physical level as well.

Through the Anointing of the Sick, we embrace a narrative that says Jesus is in our midst and we have nothing to fear because even death cannot separate us from his love. The sacrament reminds us that the sickness, disease, or injury we suffer from cannot claim ownership of us—cannot have us—because we have been claimed by Christ and belong to him. The first step in healing is to refuse to be defined by the malady we suffer. Instead, the Sacrament of the Anointing of the Sick

Through the Anointing of the Sick, we embrace a narrative that says Jesus is in our midst and we have nothing to fear because even death cannot separate us from his love.

reminds us that we are defined by our relationship with Christ: "In him we live and move and have our being" (Acts 17:28).

In the Anointing of the Sick, we encounter God in our brokenness. Our world despises brokenness and, indeed, brokenness is not something to relish. However, our faith teaches us that it is in our brokenness that we are most capable of recognizing the presence of God. This is why we keep crucifixes in our homes. We look to a symbol of brokenness to represent our salvation. It was through Jesus' brokenness and his Resurrection that we are saved. When we are broken by sin or by the burden of serious illness, we turn, in our vulnerability, to God for healing.

> **Our faith teaches us that it is in our brokenness that we are most capable of recognizing the presence of God.**

Who Is the Sacrament of the Anointing of the Sick For?

Simply put, the Sacrament of the Anointing of the Sick is for anyone suffering from a serious illness or condition. The Church's use of the word *serious* gives us direction without placing severe restrictions on the celebration of the sacrament. The rite calls for a "prudent or reasonably sure judgment, without scruple" (*The Rites of the Catholic Church, Pastoral Care of the Sick*, General Introduction, 8). In general, this means that those to be anointed may include

> those preparing for surgery
> those who suffer the weakness of old age
> children who are seriously ill
> those with chronic illness or addictions
> those suffering from serious mental health problems
> anyone else whose health is seriously impaired by sickness

Likewise, the sacrament may be repeated if the sick person recovers after being anointed but becomes ill again or if the person's condition worsens.

Living the Sacrament of the Anointing of the Sick: Healing as God's M.O.

[89]

A Catholic priest in a rural farming community got up one morning and opened his window to let in some fresh air when he noticed a donkey lying in the middle of the road in front of the church. He went out to check on the donkey and saw that it was dying. The priest called the local police chief and said, "Chief, sorry to bother you, but there's a very sick jackass lying in the road in front of the church, and I'd appreciate it if you would take care of the matter before people start arriving for Mass." The police chief, who was anti-Catholic, replied snarkily, "Sure, Father, but I was always under the impression that you Catholic priests took care of anointing and last rites and all that stuff." For a moment there was dead silence before the priest replied, "Well, we do, but we are also obliged to notify the next of kin."

Living the Sacrament: Catholics Caring for Health

While the Anointing of the Sick is a specific rite celebrated in specific circumstances and performed by an ordained priest, it is best seen as the pinnacle of the entire Catholic approach to illness—an approach that involves and indeed relies on ordinary Catholics. A discussion about Catholics caring for health is not to be confused with a discussion about Catholic healthcare, which refers to a multibillion-dollar network of hospitals. While the Catholic Church is the world's largest nongovernment provider of healthcare, a discussion of that reality lies outside the scope of this book. For our purposes, we will look at the role that caring for health plays or should play in the daily life of individual Catholics.

As we've already noted, Jesus was a teacher and a healer. It is no surprise nor is it a coincidence that followers of Jesus have long been known for establishing schools and hospitals. Even before they began establishing such institutions, however, followers of Jesus have directed their attention to teaching and caring for the sick—a focus that resulted eventually in the establishment of vast networks of schools and hospitals.

"**The care of the sick is to be placed above and before every other duty, as if indeed Christ were being directly served by waiting on them.**"
—The Rule of St. Benedict

At the heart of this care for the sick was and continues to be the recognition that Jesus did not just wave a magic wand or blink his eyes or wiggle his nose to cure people. He gave them individual attention and brought healing through his touch. This has inspired countless Christians throughout the ages to show great tenderness and care for those who are sick and, in many ways, led to the establishment of "nursing as an organized service to society" (Sr. Charles Marie Frank, W.B. Saunders, *Foundations of Nursing*).

St. Veronica

Perhaps the first model of what this kind of compassionate care looks like for followers of Jesus the Christ is embodied in the Sixth Station of the Cross: Veronica Wipes the Face of Jesus. Although this story is not found in Scripture, Catholic Tradition teaches us that a woman named Veronica courageously approached Jesus when he was on his way to Calvary, and she carefully tended his facial wounds with a cloth or veil. Because of that encounter, the image of Jesus' face was impressed upon the cloth and upon Veronica's mind and heart so that Veronica—whose name means "true icon"—could carry it with her as a disciple of Jesus. Veronica (my mother's name) represents for us the proper response to the calling to follow Jesus: we are to courageously and proactively seek out those who are suffering, show them tender and compassionate care, and allow the image of Jesus—present in those who suffer—to be impressed upon our hearts and minds.

Systematized Care for the Sick

In the New Testament, we learn that the early Church sought to systematize its care of the sick by appointing ministers to participate in the work of *diakonos*, a Greek word meaning service. The men and women who participated in this service for others cared for the needs of the poor, including those who were sick, as poverty and sickness tend to go hand in hand. These people often brought the sick into their own homes to care for them. These rooms eventually came to be called "Christ rooms," a phrase coined by St. John Chrysostom. In more recent times, Dorothy Day and Peter Maurin—cofounders of the Catholic Worker Movement—sought to recover the concept of the Christ room following the Great Depression. A Christ room is a room set apart in one's home for welcoming someone in need. While it may not be feasible in our day and age to designate a physical

Living the Sacrament of the Anointing of the Sick: Healing as God's M.O.

[91]

space in our own home for those who are sick and in need, we are indeed called to create a "Christ room" in our hearts, a space where we pay special attention to those who are sick and in need of healing.

Simply put, if you want to take a first step in deepening your commitment to Christ, you should begin by caring for the sick. It is where Christ would send you if you approached him to ask what you can do to help. I would go so far as to say that any claim to discipleship that does not place an emphasis on caring for the needs of those who are sick or poor is not a full, authentic expression of Christian discipleship. This is why one of the corporal works of mercy is visiting the sick and two of the spiritual works of mercy are consoling the doubtful (it is not uncommon for one's faith to be shaken in the midst of illness and suffering) and comforting the sorrowful (sorrow is a reaction that is not limited to death but is often present in the face of sickness).

> **Simply put, if you want to take a first step in deepening your commitment to Christ, you should begin by caring for the sick.**

Thin Moments: Caring for the Sick

For too many of us, unfortunately, the responsibility of caring for the sick has become delegated to specialists such as doctors, nurses, pastors, chaplains, and ministers of care. There are many ways, however, that we ordinary Catholics can encounter Christ by tending to the needs of those who are sick:

> when we spend quality time with those who are sick or homebound
> when we take the time to call or to send a card, a text, a tweet, an email, flowers, candy, or some other gift to someone who is sick
> when we volunteer to drive patients to medical appointments and treatment facilities
> when we volunteer at a hospital
> when we assist those who are full-time caregivers for family members
> when we cook and deliver meals to the sick and homebound
> when we take a moment to pray for those who are sick

Sickness and Suffering

Christians do not relish suffering, but neither do we necessarily seek its cessation. Instead, we seek its transformation, recognizing its reality but fixing our eyes on the possibility of new life that lies within and beyond it. The Cross and the Resurrection depend on each other: without the Resurrection, the Cross is a symbol of defeat, but without the Cross, the Resurrection could not have happened. For Christians, the path to fullness of life leads through, not around, suffering and death. It is for this reason that we seek to encounter and minister to those who are suffering and in need—not solely to ease or eliminate their suffering but also to encounter God. While we seek to reveal God's compassion and mercy to them, they reveal to us the face of God in our midst.

The bottom line is this: the Resurrection of Jesus Christ enables us to live in confident hope, knowing that we have a future that includes a renewed body living on a renewed earth within a renewed cosmos. The world around us often tempts us to despair. To be a follower of the risen Christ is to take confident hope into places of despair, especially where people are suffering from illness, so that life may be transformed and have meaning.

> **To be a follower of the risen Christ is to take confident hope into places of despair.**

Christian hope recognizes and acknowledges pain and suffering—the perceived absence of God—but believes in a future that is permeated with the presence of God. When our present is filled with pain and suffering, we become insecure and preoccupied with self-preservation. Such insecurity causes us to be fearful, anxious, and greedy—all qualities that force us to operate out of a narrow space instead of recognizing that we are in a thin space—a *thin* moment—in which God is present.

Hope, on the other hand, embraces the promise of security, which in turn expands the soul and breeds selfless love—the kind of love that reveals the face of God. Christian hope is buoyed by the seeds of a new world already taking shape in this life. It is a hope that energizes us to live differently and compels us to spread the word that life is indeed worth living. This is the kind of hope we are called to bring to those who are suffering from sickness.

Benefits of Caring for the Sick

Caring for those who are sick is not only our responsibility, it is also

> a deeply spiritual experience that brings us into the mystery of God's grace
> an opportunity to show true love and compassion and an exercise in humility because it immerses us in a situation of vulnerability—our own and that of the sick person
> a reminder to be grateful for the gift of health and to do all we can to protect and promote our own health and the health of others
> an opportunity to do unto others as we would have them do unto us
> an exercise in deepening our prayer life and an expression of faith
> an opportunity to share in Christ's ministry of healing
> an act of evangelization when we express that our words and actions toward those who are ill are inspired by faith in Jesus
> an opportunity to prepare those who are sick to celebrate the Sacrament of the Anointing of the Sick
> a reminder of the preciousness of human life

So Why Does God Allow Evil to Happen?

Sometimes, when bad things such as illness occur, we seek to console those who are suffering by saying, "It's God's will." It's not much consolation to think that God is the cause of our suffering. The truth is, God does not will human suffering. Some human suffering, such as sickness and death, is part of the human condition, the result of our fall from grace and not the punishment for any one individual's sinful life. The question remains, "Where is God when suffering is happening?" Our Catholic faith proclaims that God is present with us, just as he was present with his Son, Jesus, as he hung upon the Cross. His presence in times of suffering enables us to see beyond the moment we do not understand to a moment when we will find redemption, a transformed way of seeing that brings us closer to him and, thus, to our salvation. We human beings are communal in nature, and few moments in life make us feel more alone or isolated than sickness. It is precisely at these moments that we are called to be present so that our confident hope may rub off on those experiencing the despair of sickness.

As we encounter the suffering of those who are sick or injured, we are called to take a cue from a small group of people who stood at the foot of the Cross as Jesus suffered and died. This small group—known as the "little company of Mary"—was composed of Mary, the mother of Jesus; Mary, the wife of Clopas; Mary Magdalene; and John the Apostle. They steadfastly and courageously stood by Jesus as he suffered. They knew that, in the shadows of suffering, they stood at the intersection of heaven and earth. Their witness inspired the establishment of a religious order named the Little Company of Mary Sisters, who are committed to "pray and care for the suffering and dying in the world" in an attempt to "make visible the healing presence of Jesus in the midst of human suffering through prayer, compassion, and presence." Illness seeks to author a narrative of hopelessness, fear, and despair. It is up to us, as disciples of Christ, to proclaim a narrative of rescue, restoration, and reassurance.

> "Even the weakest and most vulnerable, the sick, the old, the unborn and the poor are masterpieces of God's creation, made in his own image, and deserving of the utmost reverence and respect."
>
> —POPE FRANCIS

Living the Sacrament of the Anointing of the Sick: Healing as God's M.O.

[95]

Scripture

Blessed are those who have regard for the weak;
*the L*ORD *delivers them in times of trouble.*
*The L*ORD *protects and preserves them—*
they are counted among the blessed in the land—
he does not give them over to the desire of their foes.
*The L*ORD *sustains them on their sickbed*
and restores them from their bed of illness.
(PSALM 41:1–4)

Prayer

God, Divine Physician, we come to you for healing. Our world, my life, is filled with examples of people suffering from sickness, experiences that often drive us to despair and sadness. Too often, when we are sick, it feels as if you have abandoned us. Help us recognize that it is in our moments of suffering that you desire to be with us most. Help us experience your nearness and bring recognition of your nearness to those on the brink of despair. May compassionate care for those who are sick become my new M.O. Help me respond to the needs of those who are suffering as Veronica tended to your wounded face as you carried the Cross to Calvary. And, as you did with her, may you impress your image upon my heart and soul. Amen.

Chapter 7
Living the Sacrament of Matrimony: Who Loves You Most?

> The entire Christian life bears the mark of the spousal love of Christ and the Church. Already Baptism, the entry into the People of God, is a nuptial mystery; it is so to speak the nuptial bath, which precedes the wedding feast, the Eucharist. Christian marriage in its turn becomes an efficacious sign, the sacrament of the covenant of Christ and the Church. Since it signifies and communicates grace, marriage between baptized persons is a true sacrament of the New Covenant. (*Catechism of the Catholic Church*, no. 1617)

Who Loves You Most?

In 2005, the Broadway musical *Jersey Boys* opened to rave reviews and went on to earn four Tony Awards during its amazing twelve-year run. The musical tells the story of the popular 1960s group Frankie Valli and the Four Seasons and their many hits, including their 1975 hit "Who Loves You?" In that song, the singer asks, "Who loves you?" followed by the questions, "Who's gonna help you through the night?" and "Who's always there to make it right?" Of course, these questions are rhetorical—a way of reminding someone that beyond any shadow of a doubt, the answer to each question can be found solely in the one asking. It is a way of asserting that "I'm the one who loves you most!"

> Sometimes, we need to be reminded of who loves us most.

Sometimes, we need to be reminded of who loves us most. In fact, British author Samuel Johnson famously said, "People need to be reminded more often than they need to be instructed." Throughout Scripture, God reminds his people of his great love for them. A closer look at the actual phrasing of the First Commandment illustrates this tendency on the part of God to remind his children of what he has done for them:

> "I am the Lord your God, **who brought you out of Egypt, out of the land of slavery**. You shall have no other gods before me." (Exodus 20:2–3)

This was God's much kinder way of telling his children, as some parents have been known to say, "I brought you into this world, and I can take you out of it!" While no loving parent actually means the latter half of that statement, the first half is a variation of "Who loves you most?"—a reminder that everything this child has was made possible by the loving act of the parent. In fact, if you wanted to paraphrase the First Commandment, the question "Who loves you most?" would suffice. Look at some other examples of God reminding his people that their very existence is owed to him.

✚ For I am the LORD **who brought you up out of the land of Egypt**, to be your God; you shall therefore be holy, for I am holy. (Leviticus 11:45)

✚ I am the LORD your God, **who brought you out of the land of Egypt**, to be your God: I am the LORD your God. (Numbers 15:41)

✚ I am the LORD your God, **who brought you out of the land of Egypt**, out of the house of bondage. (Deuteronomy 5:6)

✚ But you shall fear the LORD, **who brought you out of the land of Egypt** with great power and with an outstretched arm; you shall bow yourselves to him, and to him you shall sacrifice. (2 Kings 17:36)

✚ I am the LORD your God, **who brought you up out of the land of Egypt**. Open your mouth wide, and I will fill it. (Psalm 81:11)

To this day, God's children—the Jewish people—respond, not by rolling their eyes at God's constant repetition but by reminding each generation who loves them most. When the youngest child asks, "Why is this night different from any other night?" the answer includes the following:

> We were slaves to Pharaoh in Egypt, and God brought us out with a strong hand and an outstretched arm. And if God had not brought our ancestors out of Egypt, we and our children and our children's children would still be subjugated to Pharaoh in Egypt. (Passover Haggadah)

The bottom line is, it's always good to know who loves you most, who has your best interests in mind. You know those people because they are with you, not just during the good times but also when things aren't going well. They are with you through thick and thin. Let's see if I can find some words that are a bit more poetic. I'm talking about someone who will take you:

"to have and to hold,
for better, for worse,
for richer, for poorer,
in sickness and in health,
until death . . . "

Hmmm. Those words sound familiar, eh? Indeed, the words used in traditional wedding vows pledge a love that is steadfast and enduring. With these words, spouses assure each other that they will always have the other's best interests in mind and that, as the years go on, each one will be able to ask, "Who loves you most?"—confident in the answer.

God, Our Spouse

Obviously, I'm not the first person who thought of the similarity between God's love and the love between a husband and wife. Throughout Scripture, marriage is used as a metaphor for God's love for his people.

> **Throughout Scripture, marriage is used as a metaphor for God's love for his people.**

➕ For your Maker is your **husband**–the LORD Almighty is his name. (Isaiah 54:5)

➕ "It will not be like the covenant I made with their ancestors when I took them by the hand to lead them out of Egypt, because they broke my covenant, though I was a **husband** to them," declares the LORD. (Jeremiah 31:32)

➕ For the LORD will take delight in you, and your land will be **married**. As a young man marries a young woman, so will your Builder **marry** you; as a **bridegroom** rejoices over his **bride**, so will your God rejoice over you. (Isaiah 62:4-5)

✚ Jesus answered, "How can the guests of the **bridegroom** mourn while he is with them? The time will come when the **bridegroom** will be taken from them; then they will fast." (Matthew 9:15)

✚ Let us rejoice and be glad and give him glory! For the **wedding** of the Lamb has come, and his **bride** has made herself ready. Fine linen, bright and clean, was given her to wear. (Revelation 19:7-8)

No other Scriptural example of marriage as a metaphor for God's love for his people comes close to capturing the depth and beauty of the Song of Songs, the only book in the Bible that does not mention the name of God! If this extended love song were made into a movie today, it would be rated R because it is passionate, erotic, and explicit in its description of the love between a man and a woman, a bridegroom and his bride. Judeo-Christian tradition has included this book in the list of canonical Bible books because the entire book—and marriage between a man and a woman—is seen as a metaphor for the love between God and his people. This book reveals that the love that is found at the intersection of heaven and earth is quite passionate. I recommend you read it in its entirety—and prepare to blush at times!

A Painful Metaphor

Another Scriptural example of marriage as a metaphor for God's love for his people is found in the Book of Hosea. While Song of Songs might make one blush, the story of Hosea and his unfaithful wife, Gomer, might make one outraged. If the Song of Songs would make for an R-rated movie today, the story of Hosea and Gomer would make for a prime-time soap opera, complete with scandal and deceit. Depending on the translation, Gomer is referred to as "promiscuous" (NIV), a "harlot" (NASB), a "prostitute" (NABRE), or a "whore" (KJV), none of which suggest her to be a woman worthy of Hosea's love. And yet, Hosea is instructed to pursue and marry her, which he does. Even after having children together, Gomer has an adulterous affair. Yet, God directs Hosea to love her—to keep her best interests at heart—despite her unworthiness, just as God remains faithful to his people who have not been faithful. Hosea, in fact, "buys her back" from her lover and restores her to her position as his wife. He redeems her, rescues her, reconciles with her; he does all the things that God does for us.

God uses the rocky marriage of Hosea and Gomer to remind his people Israel who loves them most and who has always kept their best interests in mind:

> "When Israel was a child, I loved him,
>   and out of Egypt I called my son.
> But the more they were called,
>   the more they went away from me.
> They sacrificed to the Baals
>   and they burned incense to images.
> It was I who taught Ephraim to walk,
>   taking them by the arms;
> but they did not realize
>   it was I who healed them.
> I led them with cords of human kindness,
>   with ties of love.
> To them I was like one who lifts
>   a little child to the cheek,
>   and I bent down to feed them."
> (Hosea 11:1–4)

Love Rescues

We said at the outset of this book that the Judeo-Christian narrative tells the story of a God who rescues, restores, and reassures. It's interesting to note that pop songs about love often include references to the notion of being "rescued."

> The Rolling Stones sang of coming to "your emotional rescue."
> The Dixie Chicks sang of being "past the point of rescue."
> Neil Young sang that "someone's gonna rescue you."
> Ryan Adams sang of the "rescue blues."
> Numerous artists (beginning with Fontella Bass) sang "rescue me."
> Chicago sang "rescue you."

It is no secret that love, in many ways, rescues us from the pain of loneliness and despair. Many of us who are married might say that our spouses have ultimately rescued us from ourselves!

A Compulsive Desire to Pursue the Best Interests of Others

Throughout Scripture, we are reminded that God loves us most, as exemplified by his constant attention to humankind's best interests, even when humankind repeatedly fails. As followers of Jesus Christ, we are called to bring this steadfast love and goodness of God—always having the best interest of others in mind—to others. In Scripture, goodness is not measured by one's ability to simply avoid doing bad. Rather, it is an active trait, an almost compulsive desire to pursue the best interests of others, often at the cost of one's own needs. George Bailey, the character played by Jimmy Stewart in *It's a Wonderful Life*, comes to mind. He was someone who continually put his own dreams on the back burner to enable someone else to achieve theirs.

> **In Scripture, goodness is not measured by one's ability to simply avoid doing bad. Rather, it is an active trait, an almost compulsive desire to pursue the best interests of others, often at the cost of one's own needs.**

This kind of selfless love characterizes the life of disciples of Jesus. In the early Church, in fact, the term *martyr* was not just applied to people who physically gave up their lives out of love for God but also to anyone who gave witness to the Death and Resurrection of Jesus through their words and actions, which were characterized by selfless love: the "laying down" of one's own life. To lay down one's life does not necessarily mean to die physically but to set aside your own needs in favor of tending to the needs of others. Parents and spouses do this every day, which is why marriage and parenthood are seen as metaphors for God's love for his people—love that reached its climax in God's only Son, Jesus, laying down his life for us.

Whether or not we are married, the institution of marriage serves as an example—a metaphor—for the Christian life. It reminds us that anyone who unselfishly and sincerely puts the needs of others before their own, ~n when receiving remuneration, is participating in the divine life: teach-~t responders, customer service representatives, medical personnel, flight attendants, and so on. No matter what situation they ~es in, disciples of Jesus make a habit of having the best inter-~s in mind.

Thin Moments: Wedding Rings and the People Wearing Them

While the signs of Baptism—water, oil, fire, white garment—are so prominent, one may wonder what, exactly, are the signs and symbols of matrimony. Of course, there are the wedding rings; however, those are primarily cultural symbols and not officially sacramentals of the Rite of Matrimony. The actual sign or symbol are the husband and wife themselves and their public consent. We have many opportunities to be reminded of how the love of a married man and woman is representative of the love of God for his people:

> when you see a couple holding hands
> when you attend a wedding and witness the exchange of vows
> when you see elderly spouses caring for each other
> when you celebrate a wedding anniversary
> when you look at wedding pictures and videos
> when you see couples dancing arm in arm
> when you see married couples caring for their children

It's Not about You: Haven't We Heard That Before?

We have seen elsewhere in this book that the sacraments, beginning with Baptism, remind us that "it's not about you." If anything reminds you every day that "it's not about you," it's marriage and family! Matrimony is another sign of the call of all the baptized to be concerned with the salvation of others. The selfless love of a man and a woman in a lifelong commitment to each other and to the children they bring into

> If anything reminds you every day that "it's not about you," it's marriage and family!

the world is a living sign of the selfless and life-giving love that God has for us. It is also a living reminder to all of us who are baptized that we are all called to share this selfless love with one another.

So, how does one go about learning the subtleties of selfless love that make for a successful and enduring marriage? Permit me to offer three strategies that enable an individual to embrace the "it's not about me" maxim upon which a successful marriage is built—three ways to lay down your life and set aside your own needs while putting the needs of others—namely, your spouse and children, first. And, for those not married, the same strategies apply to finding true fulfillment in life!

Sharing All Things in Common and Being Blessed by Less. One of the characteristics of the early Church was that followers of Jesus shared "all things in common" (Acts 2:44), often selling

"I pictured family prayer time a little differently."

their possessions to assist those in need. They had a profound sense of stewardship, recognizing that their time, talent, and treasure did not belong to themselves but were intended to be shared. The sooner that spouses learn to become generous with their time, talent, and treasure with each other, the better chance the marriage has of thriving. While spouses do need some space and freedom lest they smother each other, the stewardship mind-set of willingly sharing what one has with one's spouse and children is the key to lasting happiness.

It is no secret that some of the biggest problems in marriage stem from financial issues and who gets to "call the shots" when it comes to financial decisions. In fact, a survey by *Money Magazine* revealed that couples fight twice as much about money as they do about sex! According to the Institute for Divorce Financial Analysts, money issues are the third leading cause of all divorces, with 22 percent of divorced couples citing money issues as the culprit. When couples unselfishly and willingly combine resources and handle debts together without keeping secrets from each other, the relationship stands a better chance of success.

Finally, more and more couples today are entering marriage already deeply in debt due to college loans for some, expensive wed- ʴing with a spirit of ing content with ʴs to the happi- ʴrriage. In *Blessed by*

"**There is no more lovely, friendly and charming relationship, communion or company than a good marriage.**"
—Martin Luther

Less: Clearing Your Life of Clutter by Living Lightly, Susan Vogt offers the following strategies for living more simply:

- eliminating clutter and excess possessions
- consuming less
- limiting time spent on social media
- giving away possessions
- simplifying your wardrobe
- limiting buying habits
- eating out less often and brown-bagging it more
- buying secondhand items
- spending more time in nature
- purchasing fair-trade products

Vogt emphasizes that living simply is a spiritual principle at the heart of Ignatian spirituality. St. Ignatius of Loyola insisted that one of the keys to spiritual wellness is detachment from the things and worries of this world that might distract us from pursuing our ultimate purpose in life, which is to deepen our relationship with God. The key to living simply can be summed up in two words: *detachment* and *generosity*. Detachment is the ability to hold on to our possessions more loosely, and generosity is the practice of sharing what we have more freely with others.

In the Gospels, Jesus does not tell rich people that they need to become poor but rather that they need to be generous in giving their riches to others. The measure of generosity is not the quantity of giving but the spirit of giving. As I explain in my book *7 Keys to Spiritual Wellness*, "Planned and habitual giving reminds us of our dependence on God, enabling us to let go of our security blankets, which provide us with the illusion of independence. Habitual giving also sensitizes us to the needs of others while acquiring possessions focuses attention on ourselves."

> **It behooves married couples to practice a spirit of poverty, which is not to be confused with being poor. It is a spirit of simplicity, detachment, and generosity.**

To summarize, it behooves married couples to practice a spirit of poverty, which is not to be confused with being poor. It is a spirit of simplicity, detachment, and generosity. Spouses are called to practice this spirit each day, recognizing that the days of owning something exclusively are, for the most part, gone. Living space, clothes, furniture, food, TVs, computers, and yes, even cars, seem to automatically become community property! It is only through detachment that we can grow closer to the kingdom of God. While society is constantly urging us to acquire more and more, detachment is the ability to say "I have enough."

Embracing Mutual Accountability. Back in the day, many men entered marriage and family life with the notion that they were the "king of the castle" who answered to no one but themselves. In almost every episode of the classic TV series *The Honeymooners*, Ralph Kramden (played by Jackie Gleason) attempted to exert his superiority and autonomy. By the end of each episode, however, all of us, including Ralph, recognized that he could not succeed without the advice, wisdom, and guidance of his wife, Alice (played by Audrey Meadows). Ralph's buffoonery skewered the notion that any one person in a marriage—usually the male—was superior or autonomous. To this day, however, couples often struggle with the notion of mutual accountability, which is one of the often-overlooked dynamics of a successful marriage.

A couple had been married for more than fifty years when the woman's husband took a turn for the worse and began slipping in and out of a coma for several months. Throughout the whole ordeal, she stayed by his bedside every single day. One day, when he came to, he motioned for her to come nearer. As she sat by him, he whispered, eyes full of tears, "You know what? You have been with me through all the bad times. When I got fired, you were there. When my business failed, you were there. When I got shot, you were by my side. When we lost the house, you stayed right here. When my health started failing, you were still by my side. . . . You know what?" "What dear?" she gently asked, smiling as her heart began to fill with warmth. The husband replied, "I think you're bad luck."

All healthy relationships rely on some degree of mutuality. Both parties recognize and share a common goal and commit to contributing equitably toward the achievement of that goal. The arrangement is not a quid-pro-quo agreement; it goes far beyond a this-for-that exchange. Instead of a mathematical trade, there is a rich and selfless sharing—a reciprocity that enables each partner to thrive and enjoy the benefits of the relationship without being depleted by constant giving and no receiving.

> **All healthy relationships rely on some degree of mutuality.**

In Scripture, especially the Old Testament, this concept of mutuality is expressed in the word *covenant*. In the ancient Near East, people entered covenants—which spelled out rights and responsibilities—to ensure that they could work together in an effective manner. For the Israelites, the central covenant was the sacred relationship between God and the people of Israel. In this covenant, initiated by God, the people of Israel had certain obligations placed on them—namely, the Torah, which includes the Ten Commandments—in return for the promise of God's never-ending presence and love. Other covenants of the time were between equals, but the covenant between God and the Israelites was not, which made it even more sacred. Their God, who was great beyond comprehension, was willing to meet them halfway, to call them again and again into his constant presence.

A marriage is nothing if not a covenant: a sacred relationship of mutuality. Without mutual accountability, husbands and wives put their relationship at risk. This mutual accountability is characterized by a "we-ness" over a "me-ness": the needs of the many outweighing the needs of the one (to borrow from Charles Dickens as well as from Mr. Spock). Marriage reminds us that we are all living on borrowed time, time that is not our own and that is meant to be shared with others. Spouses do not come and go as they please. Spouses do not keep secrets. Spouses are transparent and invite each other to have total access to their respective lives.

> **A marriage is nothing if not a covenant: a sacred relationship of mutuality.**

In successful marriages, mutual accountability becomes a way of life: decisions are made together, finances are handled together, dreams and goals are shared and discussed, schedules are coordinated, previously

Living the Sacrament of Matrimony: Who Loves You Most?

exclusive relationships become open, social media is shared, and private histories are revealed, to name a few. None of this is done to the extent that individual space is eliminated; however, such spaces (for example, the man cave) should be seen primarily as places to retreat to momentarily so as to reemerge with a renewed commitment to mutuality. In marriage, a new narrative is being composed, but it is a work that must be coauthored by both spouses and with God.

In Catholic Tradition, men and women who join religious orders take a vow of obedience, often misunderstood as forfeiting their own freedom, will, and individuality. Such obedience, however, is best understood as an acceptance of radical mutual accountability. In a similar way, married couples are called to be obedient—mutually accountable—to one another. This understanding of obedience does not mean that one spouse says "Jump" and the other replies "How high?" It means that married people are accountable to each other and to their children. Married couples have voluntarily sacrificed their exclusive individualism to live in a community—their family—which is the domestic church.

> **Married couples have voluntarily sacrificed their exclusive individualism to live in a community—their family—which is the domestic church.**

Respecting Appropriate Boundaries. We live in a time when people seem to have boundary issues. The writing of this book coincided with the explosion of accusations by women about men—celebrities, politicians, corporate executives, and other men in positions of power—who sexually harassed and/or assaulted them. Somewhere, these men, most of whom were married, picked up the notion that it was acceptable to grope a woman and demand sex from her. These are examples of blatant disregard for boundaries. However, not all boundary violations are as blatantly physical or dramatic. Sometimes boundaries of intimacy can be crossed without any physical expression at all. For any marriage to be successful, boundaries must be observed, especially regarding intimacy, whether that intimacy be physical or emotional. We often miss the intersection of heaven and earth because we stray past its boundaries in search of alternate routes.

While boundaries sound like something negative—a way of shutting others out—they are actually quite positive: a means of protecting that which is sacred. In the Old Testament, we learn that the Temple in Jerusalem was considered the focal point of God's sacred presence among his people. As such, the Temple had various boundaries that separated Gentiles, Jewish women, Jewish men, and the priests from the Ark of the Covenant, which "contained" God's sacred presence. In the New Testament, Jesus replaced that temple with the temple of his own body, and St. Paul taught that *we* are temples of the Holy Spirit. As a result, we are called to respect the sacredness of ourselves and one another. One of the ways we do this is by observing boundaries. These boundaries come in various forms.

➕ **Physical boundaries**. People who respect physical boundaries are cautious about and avoid the following behaviors with people who are not their spouse: excessive/prolonged hugging, massaging shoulders, excessive closeness, unwanted touching, sitting on a lap, unwelcome kissing, tickling, wrestling, and being alone in a private place such as an intimate bar, restaurant, office space, or hotel.

➕ **Emotional boundaries**. People who respect emotional boundaries are cautious about and avoid the following behaviors with people who are not their spouse: excessive compliments about physical appearance, intense emotional sharing, inappropriate pet names, excessive personal self-disclosure, and singling out the same individual for special duties or responsibilities.

➕ **Behavioral boundaries**. People who respect behavioral boundaries are cautious about and avoid the following behaviors with people who are not their spouse: invitations to drink, take drugs, or watch inappropriate videos or video games, engaging in vulgar language or sexual humor, inappropriate messages or photos on social media, and invitations to be alone.

> **"When you make the sacrifice in marriage, you're sacrificing not to each other but to unity in a relationship."**
> —JOSEPH CAMPBELL

The Liturgy of Marriage

The essential element in the rite of marriage is the consent of the couple in the presence of the Church's minister, two witnesses, and the congregation.

> The minister invites the couple to offer their consent, saying, "Since it is your intention to enter into marriage, join your right hands and declare your consent before God and his Church."
> The couple then publicly profess their consent.
> This consent is further symbolized by the blessing and exchanging of rings.
> Although not required to do so, Catholics are encouraged to celebrate their marriage within the Eucharistic liturgy.

In my profession—pastoral ministry—I work primarily with women, who make up probably 90 percent of the catechetical ministry. I often find myself inviting catechetical leaders and diocesan directors, mainly women, out for dinner and/or a drink to discuss our shared ministry as well as to enjoy one another's company socially. I do not espouse the belief, as do some Christians, that a married man must never dine alone with another woman. Such a notion, while noble, suggests that women are always a source of temptation and inadvertently shuts women out of many decision-making opportunities. So, while I do not agree with that approach, I do, however, believe in using discretion. My wife knows about each such dinner that I have with another woman, and the invitations are always open to others to join us if possible. Such dinners take place in public places at appropriate times so that there is no misunderstanding about anyone's intentions. While striving to use discretion, I also avoid putting women on artificial pedestals: I treat my guests with respect, whether they are male or female, observing boundaries appropriately.

Some people are more expressive than others, and their efforts may involve a lot of touching and hugging, which can easily be misunderstood. It's my job to recognize that for what it is and not to reciprocate or encourage more behavior that may cross boundaries or be misconstrued.

By the same token, I strive to be aware of those rare times when a woman crosses a boundary in her desire to express her appreciation for a presentation I have given or for one of the books I have written. Some people are more expressive than others, and their efforts may involve a lot of touching and hugging, which can easily be misunderstood. It's my job to recognize that for what it is and not to reciprocate or encourage more behavior that may cross boundaries or be misconstrued.

We live in an age that seeks to eliminate boundaries, and, while it may feel good in the moment to follow the "if it feels good, do it" mentality, in the larger scheme of things, such violations of boundaries diminish the capacity for true intimacy, which is the very heart of a successful marriage. The Church traditionally refers to this observance of boundaries as the virtue of chastity, a virtue that is often confused with celibacy. To be chaste does not mean to refrain from sex but to be faithful to one's sexual commitment, whether that is a celibate state of life or the married state.

To summarize, the key to learning how to lay down your life—to set aside your own needs for the needs of others—is to practice what the Church traditionally calls the evangelical counsels: poverty, obedience, and chastity. And you thought those were things that only religious men and women practice! While those in religious life take solemn vows to practice these virtues in a more radical form, each of us, no matter our state in life, is called to practice the spirit of these virtues. And, if you are seeking a marriage that is successful and enduring, you'll want to begin practicing these three virtues without hesitation!

The Fragility of Relationships

For some people, for a variety of reasons, divorce is the only possible recourse. Divorced Catholics often wrongly assume they can no longer receive Holy Communion. This is only true when divorced Catholics have remarried without an annulment of their first marriage. An annulment is not a Catholic divorce. It does not mean that a marital relationship did not exist, nor does it mean that the children of that marriage are illegitimate. It means that there was no sacramental bond. Once an annulment has been granted, divorced Catholics are free to have a sacramental marriage.

Marriage Teaches Us about God

Ultimately, the institution of marriage between a man and a woman is an embodiment of the love that God has for us, his people, a love that has two defining and inseparable characteristics.

First, God's love for us is unitive: it is a love that seeks intimacy. Our God's essence is one of divine intimacy; the love shared by the Father, Son, and Holy Spirit is so intimate that God is One. As creatures made in the image and likeness of God, we are called to reflect this divine attribute, something that is achieved most fully in the complementariness of a Christian marriage between a man and a woman solemnly bonded one to the other.

Second, God's love for us is procreative: it creates life. Our sacred Scripture stories of creation teach us that we human beings are not simply an accident of physics or a by-product of the evolutionary process but are the result of a specific loving act on the part of God who seeks to share the gift of life. God chose to share this power to create life with us through the ultimate act of intimacy: sexual union between a husband and wife.

It is precisely for this reason that it is the couple—not the bishop, priest, or deacon—who administer the rite of marriage to one another by expressing their consent in the presence of a minister of the Church, two witnesses, and the congregation. This consent is to give oneself fully to one's spouse, expressed in its deepest form through the consummation of the marriage. Thus, it is no stretch of the imagination to say that, for Catholics, sexual intercourse between a husband and wife is a sacrament. This outward sign of love and fidelity shared in private forms the couple themselves into a living and public outward sign of God's love and fidelity. There is no higher expression of self-giving love than the offering of one's very being—body and soul—that takes place in sexual intercourse. It is for this reason that this precious form of expressing love is to be reserved for marriage between a man and a woman.

It is because we see this union as sacred that we safeguard it. Like a priceless painting on display in an art gallery, we protect against any casual behaviors that might harm it and boldly teach that the sexual

> **"Love is our true destiny. We do not find the meaning of life by ourselves alone. We find it with another."**
> —Thomas Merton

encounter between a husband and wife is sacramental. Just as followers of Christ are encouraged to receive the Eucharist frequently as a means of encountering Jesus, married disciples of Christ are encouraged to encounter God's grace frequently through sexual expression.

Scripture

Above all, love each other deeply, because love covers over a multitude of sins. Offer hospitality to one another without grumbling. Each of you should use whatever gift you have received to serve others, as faithful stewards of God's grace in its various forms. If anyone speaks, they should do so as one who speaks the very words of God. If anyone serves, they should do so with the strength God provides, so that in all things God may be praised through Jesus Christ. (1 PETER 4:8–11)

Prayer

Lord, sometimes I really do need to be reminded who loves me most! That someone is YOU! Thank you for your steadfast and faithful love. I know I can always count on you as one can trust and rely on a good and faithful spouse. Thank you for always having the best interests of your people at heart. May I learn from all the healthy marriages that are and have been a part of my life to love more selflessly by sharing all things in common, embracing mutual accountability, and respecting boundaries. Amen.

Chapter 8
Living the Sacrament
of Holy Orders:
Helping Others to See

Through the ordained ministry, especially that of bishops and priests, the presence of Christ as head of the Church is made visible in the midst of the community of believers. In the beautiful expression of St. Ignatius of Antioch, the bishop is *typos tou Patros*: he is like the living image of God the Father. *(Catechism of the Catholic Church, no. 1549)*

What Does Priesthood Have to Do with Me?

If you're not an ordained priest, you may be tempted to skip this chapter about the Sacrament of Holy Orders. I wouldn't advise it! The truth is, everyone who is baptized into Christ is called to share in the priesthood of Christ, which means that understanding the priesthood helps each of us better understand our Baptism. In fact, in Baptism, the following words are spoken: "As Christ was anointed **priest**, **prophet**, and **king**, so may you live always as a member of his body, sharing everlasting life." As disciples of Christ, we are called to love and serve God and others by sharing in Jesus' ministry as priest, prophet, and king. But what does it mean to live as priest, prophet, and king? In short it means that

➕ as priest, we help others recognize and respond to God's presence

➕ as prophet, we speak God's truth to others and

➕ as king, we provide for those who are vulnerable

For the purposes of this chapter on the Sacrament of Holy Orders, we will focus on just the first of these three so as to arrive at a better understanding of what it means for each one of the baptized to participate in the common priesthood of Jesus Christ in our daily lives. We will also look at the role of the ministerial priesthood and how that pivotal role speaks to each of us about what it means to be a disciple of Christ.

Time for the Annual Eye Exam!

Each January, as our flexible spending accounts are replenished, my wife and I arrange our appointments with the eye doctor, an experience that is usually far more pleasing than going to the dentist or other doctors. For one thing, there is rarely any pain involved, and, for another, it is fun to select a new style of frames!

We are always so grateful for the various technicians and especially for the eye doctor who puts us through a flurry of tests and exercises that ultimately result in the satisfaction of greater visual clarity. It is always gratifying, during those exams, when they shift from a slightly blurry slide to one that brings everything into focus. Thank goodness for people who help us see.

This is primarily what a priest does. A priest is called to assist others in seeing the presence of God, a presence that is constant and yet one that too often is obstructed or out of focus and for which we need another perspective to help us recognize it. An example I like to use is the classic image depicted here that shows a woman who can be seen as either young and attractive or old and unattractive. Some people can see both immediately. How about you? If you see only the old woman, I can offer some tips to change your perspective so that you recognize the young woman, and vice versa. A change of perspective—a different way of looking at things—results in an "Aha!" moment when one recognizes something that was always there but remained hidden. The role of the priest is to transform the way we see, helping us recognize a world that is infused with the presence of a loving God and respond accordingly.

We Owe It to God

The Catholic Church did not invent the notion of priesthood. For thousands of years, human beings have designated certain individuals as priests, whose role has been primarily to do three things:

➕ represent their god to the people and the people to their god

➕ instruct others in the ways of their god

➕ preside over rituals (offering sacrifices) to honor and express commitment to their god

These three basic responsibilities can likewise be found at the core of the Catholic priesthood. All three responsibilities assist God's people in recognizing and encountering the nearness of God. In Judeo-Christian tradition, however, priests have not been defined primarily by their function or the duties they perform but by who they are on a symbolic level: representatives of a people who have been redeemed, restored, and rescued by God.

Because the Jewish people recognized God as the one who rescued them from slavery in Egypt, they felt obliged to show their appreciation and commitment. They felt that they owed it to God to give back. Traditionally, that was done by offering the first fruits of one's harvest, income, and offspring. This explains why:

➕ One entire tribe of Israel, the tribe of Levi, was designated as the priestly tribe. Although Levi was not the firstborn of Jacob, the tribe of Levi was the only tribe that did not participate in the worship of the golden calf, and thus, the special status of "firstborn" was transferred to Levi.

➕ John the Baptist's father, Zechariah, is identified as a member of the priestly tribe of Levi; John, therefore, performs the essential duties of a priest by helping people see God: "Behold, the Lamb of God . . . "

➕ Joseph and Mary brought Jesus to the Temple as an infant (Luke 2:21-40), an event we refer to as the Presentation of Jesus.

➕ Until fairly recent times, it was considered customary for Catholic parents to encourage their firstborn son to consider a vocation to the priesthood and the firstborn daughter to consider a vocation to religious life as an expression of the family's "giving back" to God in recognition of and appreciation for all the good God has done for us, not the least of which is the fact that our God has saved us from the grip of sin.

As a people redeemed, we recognize ourselves as once again having access to God. The role of the priest, then, is to remind people that God has rescued us from sin through Jesus Christ, that God is near to us through Jesus Christ and the Holy Spirit, and that each of us is, in turn, responsible to do the same for others. The priests in our midst are living reminders of the fact that we all "owe" God something—namely, the first fruits of our lives—for rescuing us from sin. This explains why, even at a subconscious level, many of us act differently in the presence of a priest; ultimately their role is symbolic, meaning that their presence reminds us of the presence of God, which, in turn, reminds us of God's wondrous deeds and the fact that we all "owe" God a worthy response.

> **The priests in our midst are living reminders of the fact that we all "owe" God something— namely, the first fruits of our lives—for rescuing us from sin.**

Oh, to Be Thin

Typically, when the topic of priesthood comes up, people start to argue about whether priests should be celibate or married, male or female. Those conversations lie outside the boundaries of this book. However, there is one requirement that I personally would like to see asked of all priests: they should be thin.

Now, before you send in letters of complaint, let me clarify—I'm not referring to their physical weight or size. Rather, I'm referring to the idea that just as a place can be considered "thin" and a moment can be considered "thin," so too should priests be people who are "thin." In other words, they are called to be people who do not obstruct our view of God but rather make God's presence more visible to us. I know some overweight priests who are very thin. By the same token, I know some thin priests who take up so much space that you can't see past them. The role of the priest is not to draw attention to himself but to the presence of God in the moments of our everyday lives: to open our eyes to recognize God's nearness so that we, in turn, as members of a priestly people, can bring others to the same type of "Aha!" moment, a new awareness and a new way of seeing.

Priests are present to us at many of the "thin moments": birth, reception of First Eucharist, success, achievement, failure, marriage, sickness, and death. At these various thin moments, there is great potential for recognizing the presence and movement of God. The priest's role is to journey with us at these thin moments and, like a tour guide or docent, assist us in understanding how God is near and active in the moment.

> "Do you wish to know if the people of any place are righteous? If you find him pious, just, sound, believe the people will be the same, for they are seasoned with the salt of his wisdom."
>
> —St. John Chrysostom

Priests do this best by being thin themselves—by allowing God's presence to be revealed through their presence, words, and actions.

The Benefits of Being "Thin"

I know that when I put on too many pounds, I find it more difficult to perform certain tasks such as running to catch the morning train before it leaves the station or climbing a flight of stairs. When I shed those extra pounds, I become more capable of successfully completing such tasks. In a similar way, when a priest's humility and compassion allow him to be "thin," he becomes much more capable of successfully fulfilling the following priestly tasks:

✚ *Priests reveal Jesus' presence to others.* Priests do not perform magic. They do not pull Jesus out of a hat. As Catholics, we believe that God is present everywhere in his creation. Through the rituals of our sacramental life, however, that presence is manifested to us and heightened/deepened.

> **Priests do not perform magic. They do not pull Jesus out of a hat.**

Through their leadership role in the sacramental celebrations of the Church and their pastoral care, priests assist God's people in recognizing the presence of the risen Christ in our midst, in good times and in bad, so that we may encounter him and enter a more intimate relationship with the Father, through him and with the Holy Spirit. The priest's role in every situation is to be *thin*—to draw attention not to himself but to the presence of the Lord in our midst. This is why the priest wears vestments; they "conceal" his personal identity and point instead to the presence of the Lord. Each of us, in our own way, is called, as a priestly people, to reveal the presence of God to others in everyday situations. We do this by exhibiting the fruits of the Holy Spirit: love, joy, peace, patience, kindness, goodness, faithfulness, gentleness, and self-control (Galatians 5:22). In essence, St. Paul is suggesting that when we exhibit these qualities and characteristics, we become "thin" and allow God's presence to shine through us.

✚ *Priests preside over worship.* We humans are created to be aligned with God. Over time, however, life has a way of wearing us down and causing us to veer off course: like a car's wheels, we become misaligned. To once again be properly aligned with God, we participate in worship. To worship (in Hebrew) means to "bow down to." Notice what we do when we bow: we physically align ourselves—we orient ourselves—with the person or thing to which we are bowing. To bow to someone or something is to say, "I direct all of my being to you." The First Commandment directs us not to bow down before any false gods but to direct our entire being to God alone. As Christians, the way we strive to keep ourselves aligned with God is through worship. As Catholics, this worship takes place through the sacraments and, centrally, through the celebration of the liturgy. The role of the priest is to preside over our worship so that we may be guided by the Holy Spirit to realign ourselves with God. At the end of the Mass, we are told, "Go in peace, glorifying the Lord with your life." Our very lives are intended to be a form of worship, living in such a way as to invite others to realign their lives, to be directed toward God who is the source of all goodness. You could say that to worship is to love, for to love is to direct all our attention, our very being, to the presence of another.

✚ *Priests offer sacrifice.* When someone invites us over to their home for dinner, it is customary and polite to ask, "What can I bring?" In this way, we acknowledge the generosity of the person offering the invitation and the effort they are going through to share what is theirs with us. By offering to bring something, we seek not only to embrace but also to deepen the relationship

"Father, does a priest have to eat his broccoli if he doesn't want to?"

The Sacrament of Holy Orders consists of three kinds of participation:

> Bishop. A bishop receives the fullness of the Sacrament of Holy Orders and is the head of a local church or diocese. He is also part of the episcopal college, which refers to the bishops of the world together with the pope. Bishops may administer all the sacraments. Only bishops may ordain priests. Ordinarily, the Sacrament Confirmation is reserved for the bishop, unless he delegates that authority to pastors such as on Holy Saturday when priests may confirm during the Easter Vigil.

> Priest. A priest serves the community in a variety of ways such as presiding at liturgies, preaching, administering the sacraments, counseling, serving as pastor of a parish, and teaching.

> Deacon. A deacon assists the bishop by serving the needs of the community, proclaiming the Gospel, teaching and preaching, baptizing, witnessing marriages, and assisting the priest at liturgies. Some deacons are transitional, meaning that they are preparing to serve as priests. Other deacons are called to remain deacons for life and to serve the Church in this capacity. These deacons may be married.

that this event celebrates and symbolizes. It is our way of showing that, like our hosts, we are putting ourselves into this experience, that we are "all in" when it comes to this relationship. This is the essence of a sacrifice: the offer to "bring something" that represents offering ourselves in response to the generous giving of another. The role of the priest is to offer sacrifice. For Catholics, this sacrifice is the Mass, the celebration of the Eucharist, which is not only a meal but also a sacrifice. God has been so good to us. Unfortunately, we have not always reciprocated. Despite this, God continually invites us to his banquet. When we stop to think of what we can possibly bring to this banquet, we realize that anything we have to offer falls short of what we truly "owe" God. Jesus offers himself to the Father on our behalf: he gives his very self—his entire being—to the Father so that we can fully enjoy the fruits of the relationship the Father offers to us. In the Eucharist, the priest presides over this offering of

Jesus to the Father. We, in turn, join in this act of self-giving by bringing something that represents ourselves and our lives: bread, wine, and material goods. God, in his great generosity, receives those gifts and transforms them into the only "food" that can satisfy the hungry heart: the gift of himself, the Body and Blood of Jesus Christ, the Son of God. Just as the priest presides over the sacrifice of the Mass, we are called to offer our lives every day as a sacrifice, an offering to God. This means that, in every encounter, we should be asking ourselves "What can I bring?" to express the giving of ourselves to those we are encountering.

✚ *Priests mediate the presence of God.* I once attended a conference where the master of ceremonies went to great lengths to draw attention to the fact that he was good friends with every speaker he was introducing. As a result, he talked more about himself than about the

---

Thin Moments: Holy Orders

The following ordinary moments in everyday life can serve as opportunities for you to reflect on the riches of the sacramental priesthood as well as our participation in the common priesthood of the faithful:

> when someone helps you recognize or see something you were missing
> when you get your eyes checked or put on your glasses or contacts
> when someone helps you see from another perspective
> when you pay back someone to whom you owed money
> when you gain access via a password
> when someone introduces you to someone else
> when you ask, "what can I bring?" when you're invited to a dinner party
> when you see someone bow out of respect to another
> when you eat a meal and pause to reflect on what died for the meal to happen
> when someone acts as a go-between for you and someone else
> when someone brings about unity
> when you see an ordained deacon, priest, or bishop "in action"

people he was introducing! The job of the master of ceremonies at such a conference is to remove any distance between the audience and the person they are about to encounter onstage. In short, they help the audience gain access to the person who otherwise might seem distant. In a sense, they "mediate" the presence of the one they are introducing. Traditionally, priests have been seen as mediators between people and the god they worship. In Christianity, however, this is tricky because Jesus Christ alone is the mediator between God and his people. Through Jesus Christ, we have full access to God. The role of the priest, then, is to remove any distance between us and Jesus Christ, our true mediator, so that we can recognize and enjoy the full access to God that we have been granted through Baptism. As members of the priesthood of Christ, each one of us is called to help others gain access to God—an access that has been provided once and for all by Jesus Christ, God's only Son.

> **As members of the priesthood of Christ, each one of us is called to help others gain access to God.**

✚ *Priests intercede on our behalf.* It is important for any business or agency to have a good spokesperson, someone who can effectively communicate the message of the entire company or agency to the public. This is much more effective than having numerous voices speaking at the same time and, quite possibly, giving different and perhaps even conflicting messages. When we gather as the Church, as the People of God, we are a diverse community of people with many voices. As such, it helps to have someone who can speak on our behalf, voicing all our collective needs, desires, hopes, fears, anxieties, and dreams. The role of the priest is to represent us to God by voicing all our prayers to which we add the word *Amen*. It is important to know that while the priest does a great deal of the speaking on our behalf at Mass, the people as a whole get the last word!

> The Lord be with you. *And with your spirit.*

> The Gospel of the Lord. *Praise to you, Lord Jesus Christ.*

> Let us give thanks to the Lord our God. *It is right and just.*

> All glory and honor is yours, almighty Father, forever and ever. *Amen.*

> The Mass is ended, go in peace. *Thanks be to God.*

The Liturgy of Ordination

The Rite of Ordination for bishops, priests, and deacons consists of the following essential elements:

> The imposition of hands: the bishop imposes his hands on the head of those being ordained.

> The words of consecration: the bishop asks God to pour forth the Holy Spirit and his gifts upon those being ordained.

> Anointing with oil: bishops are anointed with oil that is poured on their heads, while priests are anointed with oil on their hands.

Just as the priest voices our prayers to God on our behalf, we are called to intercede on behalf of others, to help them voice their needs, thoughts, and desires to God when they find themselves at a loss for words and unable to pray. When we offer to pray for others, we are offering ourselves as their proxy because they themselves are finding it difficult to articulate their thoughts to God due to the despair, grief, anxiety, or suffering they are experiencing. Likewise, we are called to act as part of God's response to those needs.

➕ *Priests manifest the mind of God.* Whenever we entrust another with delivering a message on our behalf, we take a chance. Will they accurately express the message as we intended? If not, great misunderstandings may occur. Over the long history of many world religions, priests have been seen as those who could be trusted with faithfully delivering the message of the god they worshiped. Today, we are leery of any individual who claims to speak on behalf of God as though he or she alone enjoys a secret channel of communication with the Divine. In the Catholic Church, priests do manifest the mind of God, not as the result of a personal revelation but as a faithful expression of that

A "thin" priest effectively reveals not his own thoughts and opinions but, rather, the mind of God to people in need of divine direction and guidance.

which God has already revealed to his Church. The role of the priest is to faithfully instruct God's people in the teachings of Jesus Christ and to faithfully interpret God's Word in light of contemporary experiences. A "thin" priest effectively reveals not his own thoughts and opinions but, rather, the mind of God to people in need of divine direction and guidance. Each of us, as members of the common priesthood, is responsible for faithfully communicating to others what God has revealed. We are also called to assist others in discerning the mind of God in contemporary situations, relying on the teachings of the Church and the guidance of the Holy Spirit.

✚ *Priests symbolize the unity of the Church.* Throughout history, armies have rallied under flags, emblems of their shared identity and unity. People need to know that they belong to something bigger than themselves, that they are part of a collective that embodies the guiding narrative of their lives. For Catholics, priests symbolize the unity of the Church. Pastors are emblematic of the unity of the faith in a given area. In a sense, the presence of priests, pastors, and bishops helps us know who we are as a Catholic community of faith. We're a community that embodies the sacred narrative that guides us: the Good News of Jesus Christ. Each of us, in turn, is called to embody that unity through our words and actions. No one of us operates as a lone agent, proclaiming our own "gospel" and serving only to fracture and divide people. Rather, we are members of the Body of Christ, striving to bring others into unity with the Lord who reconciles all people to himself.

A newly ordained priest was delivering his first homily and was, unfortunately, droning on and on, ignoring the training and advice he had received at the seminary in his homiletics class. A little boy was doing his best to listen but, before long, became quite bored and started looking around. When he spotted the red tabernacle lamp, he tugged his father's sleeve and asked, "Daddy, when the light turns green can we go?"

The Parish Needs a Pastor

Catholics tend to get a little antsy about vacancies. When the cardinals of the Church gather to elect a new pope, we wait anxiously for the white smoke to reassure us that "habemus papam": we have a pope. We know that something is awry unless the Chair of St. Peter is filled. In a similar way, Catholics are not comfortable going very long without a bishop or, at the local level, without a pastor. It is engrained deeply in the Catholic sensibility that we are not complete as a Catholic community until we have a pastor in our midst. I don't want to overstate this notion because several Catholic communities continue to exist and even thrive without resident pastors. However, the deeper sense is that it somehow detracts from our identity as a Catholic community not to have a priest in our midst.

When he was appointed auxiliary bishop of Los Angeles, Bishop Robert Barron explained in an interview with *Crux* that when he asked his new "boss," Archbishop Jose Gomez, what he wanted him to do, Gomez replied, "Be present to the people, give them hope, and teach them doctrine." Those three things, especially being present, sat well with Bishop Barron, who said, "I'm big on the bishop as a symbol"; this is a notion he traces to nineteenth-century German Catholic theologian Johann Adam Mohler, who, according to Barron, insisted that "you need to have a single person who symbolizes the unity of the faith in a given area.

> **When Catholics have a priest in our midst, we recognize at a deep level that we have in our midst that which defines us—the apostolic faith.**

The parish needs a pastor, because without a pastor they don't know who they are. The region, in this case, needs a bishop to know who they are. I represent the apostolic faith, I represent the archbishop, I represent the Church, and I take that really seriously, just my physical presence."

It would be easy for any one of us, including myself, to react to Bishop Barron's remarks cynically, asserting that he has an antiquated and triumphal notion of Church hierarchy or that he is full of himself and thinks little of the laity to insist that, without him and other bishops, we don't know who we are. Barron, however, is speaking on the symbolic level: when Catholics have a priest in our midst, we recognize at a deep level that we have in our midst that which defines us—the apostolic faith. This is why we expect so much of our priests and why we respond so virulently when they speak or act in ways that are not consistent with the apostolic tradition and manner. It also explains why the priest sex-abuse crisis was and is so traumatic for Catholics: not only was it a heinous crime and breach of trust at a governing level, but it decimated us at the most meaningful level—the symbolic level—because, for us, priests are symbols.

In Acts of the Apostles, we are told that the "people brought the sick into the streets and laid them on beds and mats so that at least Peter's shadow might fall on some of them as he passed by" (5:15). They knew that, when the apostle was in their midst, Jesus was most certainly in their midst. That is the Catholic way of thinking. We may have our criticisms of our priest's pastoral style, his method of delivering a homily, or his theology, but we know that, with a priest in our midst, we are complete as a People of God: we know that with the apostle in our midst—even if it's just his shadow—Jesus is in our midst and, therefore, we are rescued, restored, and reassured.

Scripture

Therefore, since we have a great high priest who has ascended into heaven, Jesus the Son of God, let us hold firmly to the faith we profess. For we do not have a high priest who is unable to empathize with our weaknesses, but we have one who has been tempted in every way, just as we are— yet he did not sin. Let us then approach God's throne of grace with confidence, so that we may receive mercy and find grace to help us in our time of need. (HEBREWS 4:14–16)

Prayer

Heavenly Father, sometimes we cause ourselves to feel so far away from you. Thank you for sending us your Son, Jesus, to close the gap so that we have full access to you. Thank you for sending so many good disciples into our lives, Lord, to do the priestly work of helping us recognize your nearness in everyday life. May we, in turn, do this priestly work for others so that none of your children ever feel distant from you. Bless and keep holy our bishops, priests, and deacons so that they may guide and inspire us to bring your message of rescue, restoration, and reassurance to the world. Amen.

Extending Thin Moments into Our Everyday Lives

Often, when we visit a place that has a profound impact on us, we bring back with us reminders, tokens, and keepsakes that help us recall our experience there, bring it into the present, and urge us on to the next opportunity to visit that or some other place that promises a profound experience. The profound experience we enjoyed at that location is not over and done with but continues to wash over us and influence our lives.

Similarly, married couples find ways of communicating love and affection for each other between those heightened moments when they can share themselves completely in sexual union. Touches, embraces, kisses, glances, texts, e-mails, flowers, chocolates, and other gifts and tokens recall the beauty, passion, and excitement of the last consummation, bring it into the present moment, and build anticipation for the next opportunity to make love.

In the Catholic Church's sacramental life, we are not limited to seven isolated moments in which we experience God's presence profoundly and then are left wanting until the next major sacramental milestone comes along. If that were the case, many of us would have used up our profound "God-moments" by the time we were seven years old! Even with the opportunity to receive the Eucharist and the Sacrament of Reconciliation as often as we want, it would be as if our experience of the remaining sacraments were over and done with—that is, unless we became seriously ill and received the Anointing of the Sick, and that's not something we particularly pine for!

So, then, how can we ensure that the sacramental life of the Church serves as a spiritual path for encountering God in daily living? This happens in two ways:

1. First, by developing a mystagogical mind and heart—the practice (better yet, the "art") of regularly pondering and reflecting on the "thin moments" of everyday life, those moments that call us back to our experience of the sacraments (such as quenching your parched throat with a cold glass of water on a hot day and recalling that the waters of Baptism refresh us daily).

2. Second, by immersing ourselves in the Catholic world of sacramentals. In addition to the seven sacraments we have explored in this book, the practice of the Catholic faith is enriched and enhanced by the reality of sacramentals: sacred signs, objects, actions, and blessings, all with biblical roots, that bear a resemblance to the seven sacraments because they flow from, and lead us, to them.

Sacramentals, which prepare us to receive the fruits of the sacraments, serve to sanctify moments and experiences in daily life, and draw our attention to God, come in a variety of forms but can essentially be divided into two categories:

✚ **Sacramental Actions**
> making the Sign of the Cross   > genuflecting
> bowing   > blessings
> folding hands

✚ **Sacramental Objects**
> rosaries   > oils
> statues   > icons
> medals   > crucifixes
> scapulars   > church bells
> holy water   > candles
> ashes   > incense
> palms   > holy cards

Sacramentals Are Part of God's Language

We have noted, since the beginning of this book, that God speaks to us using not only words but also signs and symbols and objects from the natural world. Like any good parent, God teaches us this language. And so, when Catholics use sacramentals, we are simply speaking the language

God taught us. To see the natural world as a reminder and expression of God's presence is to see the world sacramentally.

Statues, holy cards, icons, rosaries, crucifixes, and other sacred images—all referred to as sacramentals—draw our attention to God. We know full well that when we pray before a statue, we are not praying to or worshiping the statue, and we certainly do not believe the statue is the manifestation of God or of Mary or of the saints. Rather, we use the images as reminders of God's grace and presence in this world. In his book *The Long Yearning's End* (Acta Publications), Patrick Hannon, CSC, states that "to be known by the senses is to be loved. And more than anything else, God wants to love and be loved." Through Catholic sacramentality, God's love can be seen, tasted, touched, heard, and even smelled!

Sacramentals: Not Superstition or Catholic "Kitsch"

I have often done a fun and enjoyable exercise in which I ask Catholics to imagine that they have been hired as a creative consultant for a Hollywood movie, a story that needs to have a Catholic "flavor" to it. The director, being non-Catholic, has hired you to offer advice in two areas: suggestions for making the set (a Catholic home) look and feel more Catholic and suggestions for things the main characters can do and say that will make them seem more Catholic. In no time, folks come up with long lists of very creative suggestions, such as the following:

Suggestions for the Set (objects that make the home more Catholic)	Suggestions for the Characters (things to do or say to make them more Catholic)
• picture of the Holy Father • pictures of children's First Communion • rosary dangling from rearview mirror or bedpost • crucifix on the wall with palm behind it • parish bulletin on refrigerator • statuette of Mary • Jesus "fish" on car	• Pray to St. Anthony when something is lost. • Tell someone in need, "I'll light a candle for you." • Parents bless children at bedtime and when sending them off to school. • Pray grace before a meal, even at a restaurant. • Pray the Sign of the Cross when taking off on a flight.

After having fun with this exercise and chuckling at some of the more over-the-top suggestions, I go to great lengths to point out that these are not examples of Catholic kitsch (fluff that is easily dismissed) or pagan superstition but are, instead, examples of the Catholic sacramental vision, a vision of the cosmos that sees reality as infused with God's presence. Catholics wear medals and scapulars and dangle rosaries from their rearview mirrors not out of vanity or superstition but as reminders of God's ever-present grace. In fact, the *Catechism of the Catholic Church* warns us about the dangers of superstition:

> Superstition is the deviation of religious feeling and of the practices this feeling imposes. It can even affect the worship we offer the true God, e.g., when one attributes an importance in some way magical to certain practices otherwise lawful or necessary. To attribute the efficacy of prayers or of sacramental signs to their mere external performance, apart from the interior dispositions that they demand, is to fall into superstition. (no. 2111)

Wearing a scapular is no magical guarantee of getting to heaven; however, it is a practice that reminds us daily to follow Jesus as Mary did, being obedient to God's will, praying always, and tending to the needs of others. These are the activities that lead to an eternity with God.

Another Caution

It's important to understand that when we say we can find God in all things, we are not equating God with any one thing or object. A beautiful rock or crystal can reflect the beauty and majesty of God, reminding us of God's presence. That does not mean that God is in the rock or that the rock is sacred. Some current (and ancient) spiritualities claim that such a rock, stone, or crystal not only reflects God's beauty and majesty but also is a part of God and therefore possesses healing power or divine energy. This is a heresy known as pantheism, which sees God and the world as being one and the same. To find God in all things means to see the world as a mirror that reflects various qualities of God. When we learn to see this way, we develop a deeper respect for all of God's creation

> To find God in all things means to see the world as a mirror that reflects various qualities of God.

and for one another because we realize that these are all opportunities to recognize God in our lives.

Donning Your Catholic Goggles

We started this chapter by talking about visiting the eye doctor. Ultimately, the result of that visit, for people like me who need a prescription, is the donning of new lenses through which to view the world. It is up to us, then, to wear these lenses every day unless we choose to go on with limited eyesight. In a similar way, the Catholic sacramental vision is reliant upon a lens through which to view reality. This sacramental lens enables us to recognize the nearness of God in all circumstances. It is up to us, however, to wear these lenses daily. To conclude this book, here are several ways you can don your Catholic goggles every day.

✚ Place a crucifix and a Bible in a prominent location in your home.

✚ Keep a reminder of your Catholic faith (a holy card, a small icon, or a saint figurine) in your workspace and be prepared to explain its significance to those who inquire.

✚ Carry with you or wear a symbol of your Catholic faith: a saint medal, a cross, a pin, a scapular, etc. A scapular is made up of two small square or rectangular pieces of cloth, each bearing a religious image, connected by a string. When placed around one's neck, one square or rectangle rests on the chest and the other on the back. The most popular scapular is the brown scapular of Our Lady of Mount Carmel.

✚ Look at all of God's creation as sacramental. Remind yourself to look for God's presence in nature and especially in other people.

A director of religious education arranged a meeting with one of her catechists to tell her that she could no longer allow her to serve in that role. The catechist was upset by this news and asked why. The director said, "I keep getting calls from parents saying that when you don't know the answer to a question, you just make stuff up!" The catechist asked for an example. The director replied, "Well, for starters, Mr. Harper called yesterday and said that when his son Eric asked you how the Church makes holy water, you replied, 'They just take ordinary tap water and boil the hell out of it.'"

"I can't wait to see how it ends!"

- Ask yourself at the end of the day where you recognized God's presence: in people, places, events, experiences, sights, and sounds.

- Pray the Sign of the Cross at various moments of your day: as you awake, before and after meals (even in public), at bedtime.

- Pray the Rosary, knowing that the fingering of the beads is a concrete way of meditating on the events in the lives of Jesus and Mary. To learn more about how to pray the Rosary, search www.loyolapress.com.

- Consider placing in your home a small statue or figurine of a favorite saint whose intercession you seek.

- Bring palms home on Palm Sunday and place them in various locations in your home, behind a crucifix or an icon or on the rear dashboard of your car, and keep them there year-round as a reminder that Jesus is Christ the King.

- If you have children, bless them at bedtime and as they leave for school each day. Do so by tracing the Sign of the Cross on their forehead or the top of their head with your thumb. You can do the same for elderly parents at bedtime or when dropping them off at adult day care.

- Keep holy water in your home (available in all Catholic churches!) and use it to bless the home, objects (such as Easter baskets), food, and one another.

- Light votive candles to symbolize your ongoing prayer for various intentions. When someone tells you about a hardship and/or asks you to pray for him or her, say, "I'll light a candle for you," which is the Catholic way of saying "I'll pray for you."

- Burn incense to symbolize the presence of the mystery of God and the lifting up of your prayers.

✚ Save holy cards from occasions such as ordinations and funerals and pull them out occasionally to pray for the individuals they are connected to.

✚ Pray a novena for a special intention—nine days of prayer recalling the nine days that the Apostles and Mary remained in prayer in the upper room between the Ascension of Jesus and Pentecost Sunday when the Holy Spirit descended upon them.

✚ Place an Advent wreath, a Jesse tree, and/or an Advent calendar in your home during the Advent season (beginning four Sundays before Christmas). These can be obtained from Catholic Church goods companies easily located online. To learn more about these traditions, search www.loyolapress.com.

✚ Receive and wear ashes on your forehead on Ash Wednesday, the day that marks the beginning of the season of Lent. The ashes, in the shape of a cross, remind us that we are totally dependent on God's grace and that we seek to repent of sin that obstructs that grace.

✚ Eat fish on Fridays instead of meat as an expression of personal sacrifice. Meat is a symbol of abundance and prosperity, and a fish is an ancient symbol of Christ because the Greek word for fish, *ichthys* (ɪkθəs), is an acronym for the words "Jesus Christ, Son of God, Savior." This practice is done on Fridays because that is the day of the week on which Jesus made the ultimate sacrifice of dying on the Cross.

✚ For Catholics, the days and seasons of the year are sacramental and draw our attention to God. Observe the Church's liturgical calendar—the feasts of saints and the seasons of the Church year.

✚ On the Feast of Epiphany, mark the formula 20+C+M+B+ (last two digits of the current year) with chalk above the door to your home. The C, M, and B represent the traditional names of the Magi: Caspar, Melchior, and Balthasar. These initials also stand for the Latin prayer *Christus mansionem benedicat*, or "Christ bless this house." The ritual represents your wish that all who enter your home during this year will find the newborn King within. It is also a reminder to welcome all visitors with hospitality.

✚ Kneel at your bedside in prayer; this is a traditional prayer posture that expresses humility and contrition.

+ When entering a church and approaching your seat, bow to the altar or, if the tabernacle is in the sanctuary, genuflect (touch your right knee to the ground) as an expression of reverence for Christ's presence in the Blessed Sacrament.

+ During the week, visit an adoration chapel to pray in front of the Blessed Sacrament as a way of recalling last Sunday's reception of the Eucharist and building your anticipation for receiving the Eucharist the following Sunday.

The above list is by no means exhaustive but should provide you with a solid introduction to incorporating sacramentals into your daily living as a way of developing a Catholic vision: a penchant for recognizing "thin moments" that heighten your awareness of the nearness of God.

Ultimately, faith is about experiencing the nearness of God, and discipleship is about bringing that nearness of God to others, especially to those experiencing brokenness. For Catholics, God's nearness is experienced not only in prayer but also—in fact, primarily—in our sacramental way of life. Anyone longing for a palpable sense of the presence of God need look no further than the sacramental life of the Church. Through these ancient and sacred signs, symbols, rituals, and gestures, the mystery of God's presence and nearness is made manifest, providing us with the sustenance we need to go forth into a broken world and proclaim that God's healing grace is nearby and fully accessible.

May your life be full of thin moments!

> **Ultimately, faith is about experiencing the nearness of God, and discipleship is about bringing that nearness of God to others, especially to those experiencing brokenness.**

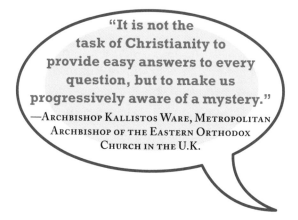

"It is not the task of Christianity to provide easy answers to every question, but to make us progressively aware of a mystery."
—Archbishop Kallistos Ware, Metropolitan Archbishop of the Eastern Orthodox Church in the U.K.

BIBLIOGRAPHY

Allen Jr., John L. "New Bishop's To-Do List: Be Present, Give Hope, and Teach Doctrine." *Crux*, August 12, 2016.

Barron, Robert. *The Strangest Way: Walking the Christian Path.* Maryknoll, NY: Orbis Books, 2003.

Bernardin, Joseph Cardinal. *The Gift of Peace: Personal Reflections.* Chicago, IL: Loyola Press, 1997.

Brandt, Willy. *People and Politics: The Years 1960-1975.* New York, NY: Little, Brown, 1978.

Catechism of the Catholic Church. Second Edition. Vatican: Libreria Editrice, Vaticana, 2000.

Collegeville Pastoral Dictionary of Biblical Theology, The. General Editor: Carroll Stuhmueller, CP. Collegeville, MN: The Liturgical Press, 1996.

de Gruchy, John. *Reconciliation: Restoring Justice.* London: SCM Press, 2002.

Dictionary of Biblical Imagery. General Editors: Leland Ryken, James C. Wilhoit, Tremper Longman III. Downers Grove, IL: Intervarsity Press, 1998.

Duke Divinity School. "Reconciliation as the Mission of God: Christian Witness in a World of Destructive Conflicts." A 2005 Paper from 47 Christian Leaders.

Eldredge, John. *The Journey of Desire: Searching for the Life We've Only Dreamed Of.* Nashville, TN: Thomas Nelson, 2000.

Fagin-Jones, Stephanie and Elizabeth Midlarsky. "Courageous Altruism: Personal and Situational Correlates of Rescue During the Holocaust." *The Journal of Positive Psychology.* Volume 2, 2007, Issue 2.

Frank, Sr. Charles Marie. *Foundations of Nursing: For the Student of Today Who Will Influence the Direction of Nursing in the Future.* Philadelphia, PA: W. B. Sanders, 1959.

Gibler, Linda. *From the Beginning to Baptism: Scientific and Sacred Stories of Water, Oil, and Fire.* Collegeville, MN: Liturgical Press, 2010.

Hanh, Thich Nhat. *The Miracle of Mindfulness: An Introduction to the Practice of Meditation.* Boston, MA: Beacon Press, 1996.

Hannon, Patrick, CSC. *The Long Yearning's End: Stories of Sacrament and Incarnation.* Chicago, IL: Acta Publications, 2009.

Healy, Mary. *Healing: Bringing the Gift of God's Mercy to the World.* Huntington, IN: Our Sunday Visitor, 2015.

Keating, Thomas. *Invitation to Love: The Way of Christian Contemplation.* New York, NY: Continuum, 1994.

Martos, Joseph. *The Sacraments: An Interdisciplinary and Interactive Study.* Collegeville, MN: Liturgical Press, 2009.

Merton, Thomas. *The New Man.* New York, NY: Farrar, Straus and Giroux, 1999.

Merton, Thomas. *Love and Living.* Wilmington, MA: Mariner Books, 2002.

New Dictionary of Sacramental Worship, The. Editor: Peter E. Fink, SJ. Collegeville, MN: Liturgical Press, 1990.

Pascal, Blaise. *Pensées.* Mineola, NY: Dover Publications, 2018.

Rites of the Catholic Church. Vatican II, Pope Paul VI. Translated by International Commission on English in the Liturgy. New York, NY: Pueblo Publishing Co., 1976.

Rolheiser, Ronald. *The Holy Longing: The Search for Christian Spirituality.* New York, NY: Doubleday, 1999.

Schillebeeckx, Edward. *Christ the Sacrament of the Encounter with God.* London: Sheed & Ward, 1962.

Schreck, Alan. *Your Life in the Holy Spirit: What Every Catholic Needs to Know and Experience.* Frederick, MD: Word Among Us Press, 1995.

Shea, John. *Stories of Faith.* Chicago, IL: Thomas More Press, 1980.

Taylor, Eugene. "Desperately Seeking Spirituality," *Psychology Today*, Nov. 1, 1994.

Tolle, Eckhart. *A New Earth: Awakening to Your Life's Purposes*. New York, NY: Penguin Books, 2006.

Twenge, Jean. *iGen: Why Today's Super-Connected Kids Are Growing Up Less Rebellious, More Tolerant, Less Happy—and Completely Unprepared for Adulthood—and What That Means for the Rest of Us*. New York, NY: Atria Books, 2017.

Vogt, Susan. *Blessed by Less: Clearing Your Life of Clutter by Living Lightly*. Chicago, IL: Loyola Press, 2013.

Vonnegut Jr., Kurt. *Breakfast of Champions*. New York, NY: Delacorte Press, 1973.

Wright, N. T. *The Challenge of Jesus: Rediscovering Who Jesus Was and Is*. Downers Grove, IL: InterVarsity Press, 1999.

Wright, N. T. *Simply Christian: Why Christianity Makes Sense*. San Francisco, CA: HarperSanFrancisco, 2006.

Also By **Joe Paprocki: The Toolbox Series**

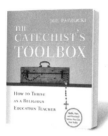

The Catechist's Toolbox

English | Paperback | 2451-5 | $9.95
Spanish | Paperback | 2767-7 | $9.95

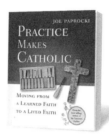

Practice Makes Catholic

English | Paperback | 3322-7 | $9.95

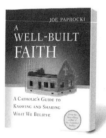

A Well-Built Faith

English | Paperback | 2757-8 | $9.95
Spanish | Paperback | 3299-2 | $9.95

Beyond the Catechist's Toolbox

English | Paperback | 3829-1 | $7.95
Spanish | Paperback | 3882-6 | $7.95

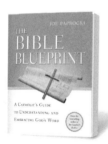

The Bible Blueprint

English | Paperback | 2898-8 | $9.95
Spanish | Paperback | 2858-2 | $9.95

The Catechist's Backpack

English | Paperback | 4246-5 | $9.95
Spanish | Paperback | 4421-6 | $9.95

To Order: Call **800.621.1008**, visit **loyolapress.com/store**, or visit your local bookseller.